ESCAPE TO HELL
and other stories

ESCAPE TO HELL
and other stories

BY
MUAMMAR GADAFFI

Introduction
by
Pierre Salinger

BLAKE

Published by Blake Publishing Ltd,
3 Bramber Court, 2 Bramber Road,
London W14 9PB, England

First published in Great Britain in 1999

ISBN 185782 346X

British Library Cataloguing-in-Publication Data:
A catalogue record for this book is available
from the British Library.

Typeset by BCP

Printed in Great Britain by
Creative Print and Design (Wales), Ebbw Vale, Gwent

1 3 5 7 9 10 8 6 4 2

Contents

Introduction vii

Part I: Novels

The City 3
The Village 23
The Earth 31
The Suicide of the Astronaut 35
Escape to Hell 41
The Blessed Herb and the Cursed Tree 55
Death 63
Jacob's Cursed Family and the Blessed Caravan 83
Stop Fasting When You See the New Moon 93
Prayer on the Last Friday 103
The Prayerless Friday 117
The Musahharati during the Day 131

Part II: Essays

Long Live the State for the Wretched! 137
Death to the Incapable... Until Revolution 151
Is Communism Truly Dead? 163
Once Again, An Urgent Call to Form a Party 181

Introduction

This fascinating book is full of information about the life, past and future, and views of Muammar Gadaffi, on the world.

As we move toward the next century, Libya, through its leader Muammar Gadaffi, is seen as one of the most dangerous countries in the world. It is seen as revolutionary, irresponsible, fanatic, and terrorist. Nations do not believe that there have been dramatic changes in the past years, and are not interested in starting dialogue with Libya. Their only interest lies in isolating the nation. And yet, there have been dramatic changes that the western world should understand.

We should look back to recent history. In April 1986, the Reagan administration decided to bomb the capital of Libya, Tripoli, to try to assassinate Gadaffi. The reason for the bombing was, according to the administration, a Libyan terrorist attack against Americans in Berlin. During the bombing of Tripoli, hundreds of Libyans were killed, including one of Gadaffi's children.

A few years later, the American and British governments, after investigations into the Pan Am 103 bombing in December 1988, decided that the bomb had been placed on a plane in Malta that connected to Pan Am in Frankfurt, Germany, and exploded over Lockerbie in Scotland. In their investigations, the two governments were aware that the bombing had been carried out by Iran and Syria. After the Gulf War, these governments wanted to see progress in the Middle East peace talks between Israel and Arab countries and the Palestinians. They decided to change their decision and attribute responsibility for the Pan

Am bombing to Muammar Gadaffi. The reason was that the Syrians, and not the Libyans, were crucial to Middle East peace talks.

I was the only one who interrogated the two Libyan suspects for planting the bomb in Malta. That interrogation confirmed to me that the Libyans had not done it, that the bomb was put on the plane in Frankfurt, and, more interestingly, I discovered that Libya had made important changes. For example, while in Libya I was allowed to visit an area that the Americans said was being used to create chemical weapons. When I went there, it was clear that they were not creating such armaments. I was allowed to visit areas where the U.S. government had proclaimed as terrorist training camps. They had been put to a stop and turned into places of residence for Palestinian immigrants. Moreover, I discovered that Ibrahim Beshari, then foreign minister of Libya, had written letters to the United Nations and to U.S. secretary of state James Baker, offering them the possibility to send in investigators to verify that what the Libyans were saying was true. Neither the United Nations nor the U.S. government replied. On the other hand, the Libyans were in touch with the British government to let them know they were ready to give important information on how, in the past, they had supported the activities of the Irish Republican Army in its military operations in Northern Ireland, although they were no longer supporting them. The British accepted the offer and learned important things through the Libyan intelligence services.

All of these views had an impact on the views of Muammar Gadaffi. In a discussion we had in 1992, he denied all of the charges against his country. He said: "Our feeling is that our country has become a victim of terror, particularly from the United States (during the Bush administration). We are starting to feel strong persecution complex from America. Libya is becoming a bottle of Pepsi Cola—they shake it and shake it until it explodes." In this book, Gadaffi makes it clear that he and his regime are totally opposed to communism. In my interview, he said that his country had never been a danger to the U.S., and in fact that they had refused to accept communism, for which the U.S. should have been grateful. In the essay "Is Communism Truly Dead?" he writes that Marxism Leninism was completely false and a dramatic mistake, and is something that has its roots in the French revolution. He denounces its origin and its methods.

Finally, Gadaffi told me: "We can go back to the language of reason and dialogue and that is also explained by the differences between presidents Bush and Reagan. As far as comparing between the attack on Libya by Reagan and George Bush's involvement in the Gulf War, there was a difference. Bush went to the world and obtained UN resolutions. He got allies. Reagan did not, convinced that he should make his own decision." Gadaffi, of course, recently said that with the second term of the Clinton administration, he was confident that there would be changes between the U.S. and Libya. In this he may not be right.

The collection of works by Gadaffi is interesting. Gadaffi's Libya has exerted much effort in making sure that an Islamic fundamentalist movement does not take power. Obviously, Islamic fundamentalism has made a strong appearance in nations bordering Libya. There is the violent civil war in Algeria, with 60,000 killed already, and the rising current of

Islamic fundamentalism in Egypt. If Libya were to allow Islamism to rise, it would explode into its neighbours and the rest of North Africa.

While other nations detest Libya, they do not understand that when Muammar Gadaffi took power he effected huge changes in restructuring the nation to make sure that there were no homeless people or unemployed or badly paid citizens. Helped along by the oil boom of the 1970s, Libya under Gadaffi has changed from a sleepy, unimportant tribal monarchy to a revolutionary third world state with a reach into other countries and continents. The country is one of the most stable in the Arab world. Actually, if Libya were not under sanctions right now for the accusation that it was responsible for the Pan Am 103 bombing, it could conceivably be one of the Mediterranean's most important tourist countries. Along the coast of Libya there are wonderful places where visitors can find historical sites and artifacts going back centuries.

Even though the great majority of the world's English-speaking population is convinced that Libya is a hazardous or unsafe country and that Muammar Gadaffi is a dangerous leader, they should read this book. It is significant because it gives a very special view about an original mentality, one that is certainly not available in the western media.

The man whom the world first came to know on September 1, 1969, when he seized the reins of power in his country, is someone who in some ways has gone through important changes, while, in others, has remained fixed in his words and deeds. There can be no argument that there is a period of considerable development separating the person who in the 1960s and 1970s used to say "joining a political party is treason" and the person who ends this book with the essay "Once Again, an Urgent Call to Form a Party."

Those who have had questions about Gadaffi will find some answers in these texts, and especially in the first stories. In these first chapters, the reader will find many instances of opposites, easy dichotomies such as the city versus the village, the earth (solid ground) versus delusion and fancy, reason versus the "blessed herb" and superstition, action versus waiting for miracles, progress versus the ways of the past.

Regarding these alternatives, we know that the author made his choices firmly a long time ago. In "The City," we find the author, who is now in his fifties, with the same opinions on the world as the twenty-nine-year-old product of an oasis environment who suddenly had the city of Tripoli and the rest of the country under the rule of his Revolutionary Command Council.

For Gadaffi, there is a fundamental difference between rural and urban life.

> The city has been with us since ages long past, but regard its plight today! ... The city was not created for luxury, happiness, or pleasure. In reality, the city is a scavenging multitude in which people find themselves out of necessity.

In villages, he sees a polar opposite:

Depart the city and flee to the village, where you will see the moon for the first time in your lives. You will change from being worms and rats, exiled from social companionship and ties, and become true human beings in the village, oasis or countryside. Leave the cemetery neighbourhoods for God's wide and wondrous land.

His enmity toward urban life is almost "holy" in nature, especially when we encounter his Quranic metaphors, describing practices such as "wa'd." This is the practice of burying unwanted newborn girls alive, to which the Quran and the prophet Muhammad put a stop in ancient Arabia. By comparing urban life to being buried alive, Gadaffi thus takes on the modern city's problems, while putting his argument in religious terms to protect himself against those who accuse him and his regime of not being sufficiently Islamic. More on that below. Gadaffi proves his fixedness, or claim to eternal truth, by borrowing metaphors from the Quran, which is, of course, God's eternally true word to believing Muslims. If the Quran, however, does not provide the precise method of comparison, he borrows from the present age and his experience. In the process, he reflects the concerns of a contemporary decision-maker:

> The city is anti-agriculture; it is built on arable land, and trees are uprooted for its construction. It tempts peasants to leave the land and become lazy beggars on its sidewalks. At the same time, the city devours agricultural production and demands more and more of it, although this agricultural production requires land and peasants. The city is anti-production, because production requires effort and patience, and the city is anti-seriousness and effort. By its nature, it wants to take and not give, consume and not produce; it stretches out in every direction, limitlessly... The city kills human and

social feelings, creating in their stead indifferent insensitivity; this is because city people have become used to the repetition of behaviour and scenes that might grab one's attention in the village, oasis, countryside, deserts.

The love of rural life is another of Gadaffi's fixed terms of reference, as a product of one of Libya's oasis towns. When we say bedouin, we should also remember that, in Libya, a good deal of bedouin life is settled, or fixed in a certain place such as an oasis, and not nomadic. But villages and oases are not merely geographical places of residence; they represent an ethic that is at odds with what Gadaffi sees as the most important types of behaviour in the city: extreme selfishness, runaway consumption, and ignoring others.

The story "The Village" is not a simplistic ode to rural life, but perhaps an unconscious response to a pressing contemporary concern. Go almost anywhere in the Arab world today and you are likely to see the effects of massive rural-urban migration over the past three to four decades. People have left agricultural regions in search of better-paying jobs in the city, although job opportunities do not always prove to be as satisfactory as people are led to believe. High population growth rates and "belts of misery" where poor suburbs have sprung up around once-calm urban centres are features of the Middle East, from Baghdad to Beirut, Cairo to Casablanca.

The story "The Earth" is addressed directly to the people of the city. In it, Gadaffi places blame squarely on urban centres, since "if we lay tile or pave it, build upon it, we will have killed it, and it will no longer give us its bounty." Of course, in Libya, Gadaffi has the luxury of taking this stance, since he rules a small population of approximately three million within a vast geographical area, although much of it is desert. Outer space, as we see in "The Suicide of the Astronaut," offers no alternative either, as it represents a dead end.

Before going any farther, I should note that the reader may be surprised by the tone of these texts. Rarely in this day and age do heads of state commit to writing, let alone publishing, their political and personal views in this form. What are we to make of this book? How can we describe Muammar Gadaffi, when we examine his writings? A basic point to remember is that Gadaffi's thought and style spring from three main influences. A few words about each source of inspiration are in order.

First of all, Gadaffi is firmly grounded in Arab Islamic culture and traditional, religious-based thought. The Quran and Islam are among the basic sources of inspiration for much of the text, although they are not the only ones. Although this is obvious in stories such as "Jacob's Cursed Family and the Blessed Caravan," or even "The Musahharati during the Day," it also appears in many other stories and essays. But Gadaffi is fighting two battles here. On the one hand, the works are firmly grounded in Islam. At the same time, they mock, sometimes playfully and sometimes crudely, the more extreme elements of contemporary political Islam and Islamist movements.

In one sense, Gadaffi is protecting himself

from any criticism by Islamists in Libya or elsewhere by showing that his learning and core beliefs spring from Islam and the Quran. But he also lashes out mercilessly at contemporary Islamists, using mockery and other devices that few Arab or Islamic leaders would contemplate in contemporary circumstances. One would have to go back to Habib Bourguiba, the president of Tunisia until the late 1980s, to find another example of an Arab leader whose rhetoric took on Islamists and fundamentalists without flattery or fine words. As I will note below, Gadaffi also attacks the leadership for the choices it made after Iraq's invasion of Kuwait. Thus, regarding Islam, Gadaffi has "enemies" on both sides—the conservative Gulf regimes, which rule in the name of Islam and applying the Sharia (religious law), and the opposition Islamic fundamentalist group seeking to overthrow Arab states, in the name of Islam and applying the Sharia.

A second source of inspiration for Gadaffi is the modern age's polemical philosophers, essay writers, and aphorists, such as Friedrich Nietzsche and others. The title of the essay "Death to the Incapable... Until Revolution" is not the whole story then:

The truly strange thing in your lives is that you not only fail, but fail to learn your lesson. Any effect on you is not taken advantage of as a useful experience, no matter how much you fail you never change. No matter how much your beliefs betray you, this is never accepted by you. You are distinguished by your inability to recognize the truth, no matter how irrefutable.

Here we have Gadaffi as late-twentieth century analyst. What is truly worthwhile, according to our author, is to improve oneself by learning from experience, making oneself stronger. Leaving the city and its spiritual pollution for the healthier countryside is also logical advice in this way of thinking. In the spirit of the modern age, Gadaffi has no problem with mocking conservative Islam when its adherents are not seeking to better themselves. Education in technology and science, and not memorizing ancient texts, is the way to self-improvement and a stronger nation. In "The Blessed Herb and the Cursed Tree," he mocks the neglect of modern progress: "Truly, what need have we of medicine factories in Rabta and Ras Lanouf as long as we have Hajj Hasan and all of his herbal medicines...?" And as he says in "Prayer on the Last Friday":

> Perhaps some of you might ridicule my argument as blasphemy or apostasy, but which person in his right mind, living on the brink of the twenty-first century, would not be alarmed by these critical issues?

Gadaffi sarcastically notes the importance of the "critical issues," which are whether one should use three or five fingers when eating. This might have been a concern centuries ago for some religious philosopher, but not for Gadaffi in today's Middle East. Nietzsche is not the only influence, because in "Escape to Hell" and "Once Again, An Urgent Call to Form a Party," we see much of Freud and psychological preoccupations. This makes sense when we remember that Gadaffi's regime is unique—certainly among Arab countries, and probably in the wider world—for its decentralized structure, based on people's congresses, people's committees, and revolutionary committees. Gadaffi's Libya is one that depends on a charismatic leader, since the army does not rule and there is no institutionalized one-party state. The ideology comes from Islam and Gadaffi's Green Book, and Gadaffi's relation with the population, is fairly direct. Thus, he addresses the concept of "the people," and, more interestingly, his relationship with them. It is not always peaceful or untroubled.

In "Escape to Hell," we are told the story of a man who does himself a disservice by coming to the city. It is there that he meets the tyranny of the mob. Strangely enough, this mob-collectivity takes on a Freudian face with Gadaffi's statement, "In the same way, I both love and fear the masses, as I love and fear my father." And more tellingly, Gadaffi notes the ultimate fate of populist leaders and figures from history such as "Hannibal, Barclay, Savonarola, Danton, Robespierre, Mussolini, and Nixon."

The third current of influence in this book is Nasserism, or the Pan-Arab ideology of unity and nationalism that reached its heyday in the 1950s and 1960s. Some have called Gadaffi the Arab leader who has clung most openly to the doctrines of Pan-Arabism. This influence is evident in the harsh analysis of "Prayer on the Last Friday" and "The Prayerless Friday," where Gadaffi angrily but almost wearily explains how non-Arab Islamic nations cannot be expected to consider Israel as the most dangerous threat to national security. Two states with Muslim populations—Indonesia and Malaysia, might be at odds with each other, while Muslims in Pakistan see India as their biggest danger. These divisions in the Islamic world, Gadaffi explains, are what prevent a united stance against Israel, which can only reinforce his belief in Arabism.

But although it is Egypt and Jordan that have signed peace treaties with Israel, in this collection we see a special attack on the Gulf states, for allowing western and other foreign forces to play the chief role in defence after Iraq's invasion of Kuwait. In "Stop Fasting When You See the New Moon," we see that the Gulf War, which may have faded from some western memories, is a watershed in the Arab world. Saudi Arabia is ridiculed for its allowing foreign, non-Islamic troops to help in the defence of a country that bases the legitimacy of its political regime on its guardianship of the holy cities of Mecca and

Medina and its supervision of the pilgrimage, the hajj, every year.

The environment that Nasserism grew up in was the third world revolutionary period during the first two and a half decades of the cold war. But this influence does not only involve Arab unity or mobilization against Israel. In the story "Death," a western reader might wonder about the significance of dwelling on battles that took place at the edges of a second-rank empire (the Italian fascist state) during the interlude between world wars. But in Libyan history and memory, one should remember that these were cataclysmic times, when approximately twenty-five per cent of the population of the time was wiped out struggling against Italian colonial rule. One should also remember that no pressure group or justice tribunal takes up this period in the court of world public opinion today.

All three currents combine in "Long Live the State for the Wretched!" in religious terms, the victory of the weak and wretched will see them triumph over the powerful, and Gadaffi borrows much from Quranic verse in this essay. While there is no direct reliance upon Arab nationalism, the call to arms does remind one of the heyday of revolutionary third-worldism. Finally, one should not forget the influence of modern philosophy, although Gadaffi has turned Nietzsche on his head—it is not the weak who resent the strong:

> This is the true secret for their hating you: you are not of this world, you are not wealthy, and for this they hate you. You are not oppressors, and for this they hate you. You are not pretenders, so they hate you. You are not hypocrites or liars, and for this they hate you.

Other contemporary concerns are addressed in the essay section of the book. The fall of the Soviet Union and its Marxist underpinnings have been on the minds of many, but Gadaffi is one of the few world leaders to have published his analysis of the question, and in it he stakes out his usual, unconventional position: communism did not die because it has yet to be born. This is defensible enough, but slightly odd coming from someone so adamantly opposed to that ideology.

At the end of the collection, we arrive at a solution: a party that is not strictly permitted according to Gadaffi's ideology. And perhaps this contradiction is where one should focus. A call to form a party is actually a call to form a people. What determines the concept of "the people"? Can it be trusted? What are the disloyal elements? Gadaffi is not known for being an ultra-nationalist, so what does he want? Taken as a whole, the author has given us a vital image of the times in which he lives. Political life in his country is torn between the overlapping crosscurrents of Arab nationalism, Islam and religion, state-building in the third world, the need for material progress, and the disappointment with urbanization. We see Gadaffi's criticism of the west for producing impersonal, dehumanizing societies, along with his admiration of its technological progress and efforts in education. We see his pride in his own history and culture, along with a harsh criticism of its less progressive aspects. This is what the book is about.

In conclusion, western audiences have seen Muammar Gadaffi as provocative, defiant opponent of United States foreign policy, Gadaffi as prophet, and we now see Gadaffi as writer and essayist. The book is composed of two sections. The first contains a group of short stories published in 1993 in Sirte. The original printing of the book included cover art of the naive school, and the "short stories" are of a genre closer to philosophy than to standard literature or politics.

The second part of the book is a collection of four essays published in Libya in 1995 by the Public Company for Paper and Printing in austere form. The slim volume bore the cover slogan "Illegal Publications." Though full of poetic flourishes in places, the essays are almost entirely political, with occasional veering off into polemic and surrealism.

Translating Gadaffi's stories and essays is an extremely difficult task, but not because of standard linguistic problems. Although the differences between Arabic and English may be great, rendering Gadaffi into a foreign language involves dealing with his underlying framework of cultural reference, much of it religious and based on the Quran. Gadaffi's work is a collection of texts that are deeply Islamic, deeply Arab and Arabic, and deeply Bedouin.

In the text, the translator has provided numerous footnotes in order to help the reader, but often in an indirect way. The references themselves are often implicit ones—to the Quran or to the Sunna (tradition of religious orthodoxy), which an Arab or Muslim reader would be likely to recognize immediately. The footnotes are also designed to remind the foreign reader of the religious and cultural resources from which Gadaffi draws. It is the translator's hope that some of the difficulties in appreciating the essays and stories have been reduced through explanatory notes of this kind.

PIERRE SALINGER

Part I

Novels

The City
The Village
The Earth
The Suicide of the Astronaut
Escape to Hell
The Blessed Herb and the Cursed Tree
Death
Jacob's Cursed Family and the Blessed Caravan
Stop Fasting When You See the New Moon
Prayer on the Last Friday
The Prayerless Friday
The Musahharati during the Day

The City

The city has been with us since ages long past, but regard its plight today! It is a nightmare and not a bringer of pleasure, as one might think, or else it would have been designed thusly. The city was not created for luxury, happiness, or pleasure. In reality, the city is a scavenging multitude in which people find themselves out of necessity. People have not come to live in the city for the sake of enjoyment, but to make a living. One engages in greed, toil, and is beset by want... it is employment which forces one to live in the city.

The city is a graveyard of social connections and relations. Whoever sets foot in it will be forced to swim over its waves from one street to another, from one quarter to another, from one job to another, and from one friend to another. Because of the nature of the city, one's purpose in life there becomes self-interest and opportunism, and one's behaviour becomes hypocritical. The Quran says: *And of the people of Medina, some are stubborn in hypocrisy.*[1] Thus, everything comes to have its own specific price in material terms, which is something required by city life. The more the city progresses and develops, the more complicated it becomes. Common friendliness and social ties become increasingly remote, to the degree that people living in the same building do not know one another, especially when the building grows so large that it becomes a mere number. People are no longer referred to by their name or the tribe to which they belong, but by a number. City people do not address one another as fellow social beings or even human entities, but as "You, who live in apartment number x on floor number x... telephone number x, license plate

1.   Quran, Sura 9, verse 101. Medina in Arabic refers to the city in the Hijaz, as well as meaning "city."

number on car is x" and so on.

Inhabitants of the same street do not know one another, since, after all, they have not chosen to live with one other. They have merely found themselves by chance living in the same street or lane, or apartment building, with no kinship or other connection between them. On the contrary, in the city the law of necessity separates relatives from one another, fathers from their sons, mothers from their children, and sometimes husbands from their wives. It gathers opposites as well as outsiders, bringing rivals together while scattering relatives.

Life in the city is merely a worm-like, biological existence where man lives and dies meaninglessly... with no clear vision or insight. In either case, he is inside a tomb, whether he is living or dying. There is no freedom or rest in the city, or peace of mind. Instead, there are walls upon walls, whether indoors or outdoors, in apartment buildings, in the street, or in places of work. You cannot sit the way you would like, walk in the direction you want, or stop when you want. If you should stop to shake hands with a friend or relative whom you have run into by accident, a stream of pedestrians pushes you along, away from him, or may hinder physical contact between you in some way. The hand that you extend to greet him with will have been pushed away by a passerby, who is unaware of what he is doing or does not appreciate the situation. If you should desire to cross the street, this will not be easy either. You may lose life or limb merely by doing so, if you do not take the proper precautions. Look to your left and your right several times. You may be surrounded in the middle of the street, so stay in your place amid the city's dangerous waves of cars, trolleys, cleaning trucks, etc., circling around you.

It is not likely that you would have the time to engage in social conversation amid the urban crowds. If such a thing does happen, it tends to be either insufferably boring or hypocritical. In the city streets, men and cats are equal... among the traffic, roads, and sidewalks. When you hear the brakes of a car, you suddenly stop and say automatically, "It's a person or an animal." This is because this is what happens when either is crossing the street in front of you. You would brake in the same way to avoid hitting either one of them. Even a traffic policeman will warn you, whether verbally or in writing, about accidents that are caused by a man—or a cat—crossing the street in the city.

This is the city. No one says "after you"; instead, they push. Push with their shoulders and their hands, push money from your pocket, push out any type of social consideration. It is "push" in the city, and not "after you." Walls respect you more than people do; at least you may gain some support from them. Walls can guide you to where you are going, after signs and instructions have been put up, while it is very difficult for a city dweller or stranger to give such information to people who are in need of it.

If you ask someone in the city for directions, he will say: "I'm sorry, I don't have any time... Sorry, I'm in a hurry... Excuse me, I'll miss the train... the bus... the car..." He may add, "The wall, have a look at the wall." The wall is the only thing stationary in the city, and people certainly cannot stand as still as a wall. In the city there is smoke and filth; there is humidity, even if it is in a desert. Your collar becomes black, even if you are a white-collar worker. Your clothes would become dirty and stained, even if you are not a painter or a repairman. As a side-effect of living in the city, you are forced to accept the filthy dust and smoke; you break out in a cold sweat, perspiring even if you are not working. You also find that in the city, you have picked up some superficial words, expressions, and gestures that are a necessary means of communication in the city, and a way to help yourself get by. You have also picked up some ready-made responses to likely questions, which you answer without paying attention too closely: no problem... no problem... an act of God... that's the one... no, uncle... no, brother... so they said... that was ages ago please, keep walking... let me through... stay away.

But whether it is you or someone else who asks you what you said just a moment ago, you would not be able to give an answer. You would not remember that you had used these expressions, because this is the nature of the city. These expressions are used automatically, to show that life in the city is ultimately meaningless, and devoid of content. What is it that is "no problem"? And who is your "uncle," or your "brother"? What is it that "they said," and who are "they"? At what time? What was it that was "ages ago"? Which way should you take in the city? If you were surrounded by such questioning, you would drown in it, unable to give an answer. It is city talk, a way of getting by and passing the time. Truly, city life means just wasting time, until another time comes to pass... a time for work, for sleep, for sleeplessness.

The city is a fad, a shouting, bedazzlement, stupid imitation, damned consumerism. Making demands while not giving anything in return, a meaningless existence. What is worse is the inability to resist life in the city. City inhabitants are unable to resist fashions, even if they do not like them. There is no ability to resist the movement toward loss or voracious consumption. Even if you are an intruder, a recent arrival in the city and not one of its original inhabitants, who have become used to its ways, you will in the end become its laughing-stock. If you wish to maintain what you believe in, maintain your values and your non-urban behaviour, you will become an outcast and find no one who understands you. When you change, though, in order to become urban, you will become awkward and fatuous.

In the city, a son might accidentally kill his father, or a father his son, while speeding along in a truck, car, or some such vehicle. It is the speed of the city, the traffic, the selfishness. The son may curse his father without knowing it while pushing him aside on the sidewalk or blinding him with his headlights in the road. Moreover, it often happens that people who should not come into contact with each other on religious grounds do so because of the crowdedness of the city. They meet, and then part, unconcerned by it all.

It is not, however, the fault of city dwellers. People are the same whether they are in the city or the village; they are practically similar in all respects, in their values and morals. This is especially so for those of the same people, or religion. Thus, it is the fault of the nature of the city itself, since it forces people to automatically and gradually accommodate themselves to life there. With the passage of time, it becomes customary behaviour. People build cities out of necessity, but cities then become unavoidable nightmares to those who built them and live in them. Everything in the city has a price, and every luxury becomes a necessity, and each price has its own material or moral price. This is where the crisis of urban life begins.

The city is anti-agriculture; it is built on arable land, and trees are uprooted for its construction. It tempts peasants to leave the land and become lazy beggars on its sidewalks. At the same time, the city devours agricultural production and demands more and more of it, although this agricultural production requires land and peasants. The city is anti-production, because production requires effort and patience, and the city is anti-seriousness and effort. By its nature, it wants to take and not give, consume and not produce; it stretches out in every direction, limitlessly. It becomes a parasite to everything around it, spreading its poisonous tentacles, killing fresh air by turning oxygen into carbon dioxide, which is then turned into carbon monoxide. Nature is disfigured, its clear mirror blurred. The city produces gases, smoke, and fumes, polluting everything. The stars and the moon and even the sun become hidden. The city coos, shouts, roars, and growls until the noise becomes deafening, and causes headaches, tension.

It spreads out and devours arable land and the surrounding villages, enveloping them under its dirty, stifling wings. Its teeth carve out roads, buildings, and public utilities from the peaceful and secure remote villages. Suburbs are formed; they start out at the edge of the city, and then become indispensable parts of it. They are ground down by the weight of the city, changing from cohesive, productive, peaceful villages into gloomy, unhealthy cells, a part of an oppressive, sick whole, which is busy but unproductive, tiring but jobless, and finally... aimless.

The city kills human and social feelings, creating in their stead indifferent insensitivity; this is because city people have become used to the repetition of behaviour and scenes that might grab one's attention in the village, oasis, countryside, deserts. In the city, you do not ask nor are asked about people moving quickly or gathering, moving slowly or dispersing. You are used to seeing such things. They do not attract your attention or make you curious enough to ask. Things like a fight, someone crying or falling down in the street, a fire breaking out—as long as it is not close to your house—or walking past tramps and the homeless lying on the sidewalk, standing against walls, or tree trunks. They might address you and put out their hands, hoping to get money from you, but this scene is so often repeated in the city that one fails to take notice. Scenes like this become the scenes that complete your vision of the city, and do not attract your attention. And even though at first they may have caused you to pause, or try to affect the situation you were observing, life in the city does not permit this.

Someone who attempts to get involved in such things cannot live in the city. Such things happen regularly, and if one pauses to attend to such things regularly, one will be constantly busy with them. Since city dwellers are many, and are made up of many groups and social and cultural levels, and because the ties and social relations that bind them disintegrate due to the nature of city life—because of this, one does not even know who his neighbour is. People are busy, they move frequently, and no one chooses to live near anyone else. Thus, people whose pains or joys you might have a notion of sharing are in fact unconcerned with yours, so how can you be concerned with theirs?

For this reason, the city has delegated responsibility for treating these issues to urban associations and institutions. A fire is none of your business, but is the responsibility of the fire department. This is the justification for a city dweller to ignore fires blazing away here and there—the fire department is responsible. I'm not a fireman... I'm busy.

Beggars are the responsibility of social associations. If I give to every beggar whom I run across in the street, I would spend everything I have on them. So, the issue is not just the beggar in front of me, but all of them; therefore, I will not pay them any attention. But what if he is truly in need? He might, however, just be lazy, or pretending. Do not let appearances deceive you, because the city is made up of deceptive appearances, and the inner truth remains hidden under the exterior form. A fight is the police's responsibility; I am not a policeman, and will not intervene. Even when honour is at stake, city people act indifferently—"that is the responsibility of the religious authorities or the vice squad, or a religious association." If you stop at the scene of a fire or a brawl, or at seeing a beggar or someone crying—and these scenes are repeated every day, and in every part of the city—could you ever reach your destination or make it back home? Do you have the ability to treat such problems?

Thus, one gradually becomes indifferent to such scenes and convinced that one is not responsible. In any city in the world it would become silly not to behave indifferently. An employee would be fired if he were to go out of his office to give aid to someone who had been run over in the street—fired for leaving work and intervening in an area outside his area of specialization (being that of the police and the emergency medical team). None of those urban associations would thank you if you were to volunteer to try to help them. They would become sensitive about what you were doing and become jealous, because you would be competing with them in the area from which they make a living.

This is the city: a mill that grinds down its inhabitants, a nightmare to its builders. It forces you to change your appearance and replace your values; you take on an urban personality, which has no colour or taste to it. No smell, no meaning—a worm-like existence. "Biology" forces you to inhale the breath of others, about whom you do not care. You attempt to protect yourself from them, rather than them protecting you or you protecting them. The city forces you to hear the sounds of others, whom you are not addressing. You are forced to inhale their very breaths; you hear the sounds of engines, motors, and hammers going along at full blast, but at a conscious level you are unconcerned by these sounds.

Children are worse off than adults. They move from darkness to darkness; from three darknesses to the fourth, as in the Quran. In the city, houses are not homes—they are holes and caves, made drafty by the movement of air from city streets and alleyways. People there are exactly like snails in their shells, protected against the waves and currents of the sea.

The city itself is a sea, with currents and waves, flotsam and jetsam... and snails. The snails are people and their poor children, against which everything in the city presses. Their parents press them further inside the shell, fearful of what awaits them in the current of the city streets. It is no use to cross this street, since there are other snails, caves, and petrified shells on the other side. Where are you going, you young and innocent children? Those are people's homes, and you do not know them. The ones who were there have moved; these are new people. The street does not belong to you alone; it is for traffic also. The street is not for playing in, and it oppresses you as well.

Yesterday, a young boy was run over in that street, where he was playing. Last year, a speeding vehicle hit a little girl crossing the street, tearing her body apart. They gathered up the limbs in her mother's dress. Another child was kidnapped by professional criminals. After a few days, they released her in front of her home, after they had stolen one of her kidneys! Another boy was put into a cardboard box by the neighbourhood boys in a game, but was run over accidentally by a car.

Go back indoors, to the darkness, to the cold and drafty or hot and dirty holes. God help the city, so full of filth. Do not think of trying to play next to the street, where there is nothing but dirt and rubbish. When all paths become closed to children, in frightful fashion, with the threat of death by being run over, torn to pieces, kidnapped and having a limb amputated or an organ removed, the least of the dangers that wait outside are dirt and filth. This is easier to take than confinement and boredom in dark houses. But the result is still death, albeit in a different way.

The sea of the city is like any other sea, and has its whirlpools and dangerous creatures, so how can a child live there? But they are there. What is the solution? The solution is to oppress children, punish them, and force them to remain holed up, isolated, and broken-down. Crush their natural course of growth, deprive them of sunlight and fresh air. This is life in the city: standing in line, get in and out of your car, no one outside your door is your friend. Even kindergarten means standing in line, filling out forms, going through formalities. The school, the hospital, the market... they are all a case of open, push, close, line up, hurry up. Children grow in biological terms, but in social terms, they are receptacles for all of these forms of repression and oppression, rebuke and reproof. They become a model of the human being afflicted by complexes and psychological problems, regression, depression. This is the reason for the decline of human values and social ties, indifference toward others and the lack of friendliness and cordiality, and jealousy.

The village and the countryside, however, are another world, different in both their inner and outer aspects. In these places, there is absolutely no need for pressure and oppressiveness. Natural growth and living in the sunlight are encouraged, if not glorified. You do as the birds and flowers do, flying and opening up to the world. There are no streets, no piles of garbage, no unfamiliar faces. People in the village and the countryside will always remain linked by social bonds, connected in all moral and material matters. Children are free to have fun and grow, they are children of the sun and moon, or breezes and winds. There is no fear of going out into the world, where there are no dangerous currents. No "open" and "close." Everything is naturally open.

There is no need for locks in an environment in which plants and children grow; there are no restraints, and no mental disorders.

O wise, kind-hearted people..., humanitarians: have mercy on children, and do not deceive them by making them live in the city. Do not let your children turn into mice, moving around from hole to hole, from sidewalk to sidewalk. The inhabitants of the city are truly hypocritical when they pretend to show their children love. At the same time, they create cages to keep their children's lovely voices far away from them, separate from their very parents. The nature of urban life for parents forces them to devise ways of keeping their little ones distant from them. This is so that they can devote their time to withstanding the nightmare of city life; by searching for, creating, and spending money on activities which neither give nourishment or satisfy hunger: false occasions, artificial parties, insincere friendships. Children are an obstacle to parents' involvement in such things. Parents take part as an effort to accommodate themselves successfully to the hell of city life. Nursery schools, child care centres, playgrounds, and even schools are ways of getting rid of children, these innocent creatures, a modern way of burying them alive![2]

2.   A reference to the ancient Arabian practice *wa'd*, of burying unwanted female babies alive, frowned upon in Sura 81, verse 8 of the Quran.

The city is harsh and fatuous for its poor inhabitants, forced to accept the ridiculous. They accept, swallowing and digesting these things as if they are quite reasonable. The best evidence of this are those silly interests which the city imposes upon its inhabitants. You find thousands upon thousands watching a cock fight—and what about the millions who follow 22 people running around meaninglessly after a watermelon-sized sack? In another silly, urban-type traditional exercise, the same crowds of people sit around a single person repeating almost inaudibly the same lines, like a parrot, accompanied by a noisy instrument, whose sound most of the audience cannot appreciate. One idiot or drunkard begins to applaud, and is then followed by the entire uncomprehending audience, as an expression of their appreciation of the exercise, which is in fact not the case, since they did not understand it to begin with. A type of affected, modern hypocrisy, which people are forced to engage in as city dwellers.

Millions of people sometimes watch another type of fight, this one between two mature people, in which they beat each other savagely; no one thinks to intervene and separate them so as to stop the brutal battle, which is in fact within their power. But modern city life prevents them from doing this, because a bloody, nonsensical battle such as this is an end in itself; this barbarism is what is demanded by living conditions in the city. Other examples are the abuse of animals in exhausting races and exploiting their blind instinct when setting them at each other in fights; the torture of people as well, hurting them and using their pain as a source of entertainment; betting on the result... these are all ways of false entertainment in the city. Unjustifiable battles between two wrestlers or fighters. After investigating these activities, one finds that there is no antagonism between the participants; it is merely something that is required by modern urban life!

The Village

Flee, flee the city, and get away from the smoke. Get away from the choking carbon monoxide, from the poisonous carbon monoxide. Go far away from the sticky humidity, and away from the poison gases and inactivity. Flee from the lethargy and waste, the poison and boredom and yawning. Flee from the nightmare city. Pull your bodies out from under its oppressiveness. Liberate yourselves from the walls and corridors, from the doors that are locked in your face. Rescue your hearing from the commotion and uproar, from the willy-nilly shouting, ringing of telephones and doorbells, from the roaring of engines. Leave the irritation behind, the anxious places, the sealed locations. It is a place of short-sightedness and wastefulness. Leave the rat race, and the rat holes as well. Leave the worm-like existence behind.

Depart the city and flee to the village, where you will see the moon for the first time in your lives. You will change from being worms and rats, exiled from social companionship and ties, and become true human beings in the village, oasis or countryside. Leave the cemetery neighbourhoods for God's wide and wondrous land. You will see constellations in the sky that will make you despise the chandeliers made of sand that used to hang above you in the city. Artificial things, which could be broken or go to waste at any moment. Dirty things, covered with flies and spiders in the burrows of the city, which are known as apartments and homes. In the countryside, look up and see the divine lanterns suspended in the dome of the sky, and not the ceiling of a filthy tomb in the city.

The village is peaceful, clean, and friendly; everyone knows everyone else. People there stick together through thick and through thin. There is no stealing in the village or countryside; everyone knows everyone else. One takes into account the reputation of his family, his tribe, and himself before doing anything that might cause harm. Any bad deed committed there does not end on the same day, as in the city, where crimes are often committed against people not known by the criminal, since there are so many people of different types and kinds there. It does not even end when it ends, but lingers on with its family, its group, its tribe, for the remaining groups and tribes, constituting a permanent disgrace for the one who committed it. This social deterrent is stronger than any civil law or city police force. Moreover, social solidarity and networks in the countryside and village take care of the needs of the needy, and prevent them from having to beg or steal. Rural life is simple, humble, and satisfying, far removed from the desires and luxuries of city life. A village-dweller does not feel the need for these silly desires which city dwellers do. The village and the countryside do not know fads and fashion; they are of calm and peaceful temperament, and are not about to change. Villagers do not suffer from tension and complexities, or lusting after wealth.

Thus, their lives are calm and easy, innocent of any pains of desire.

These desires are, of course, enjoyable in and of themselves, but they are preceded and followed by many pains and troubles. They are the pains of wanting to obtain something unnecessary, precisely because it is desired. In fact, harvesting and plowing for the sake of one's daily bread and planting trees and picking their fruit to eat are necessary things. At the least, the work that precedes them does not cause psychological anguish; rather, it is enjoyable labour because it is righteous and truly necessary. No regret either follows or precedes this work; instead, it is preceded by joyous hopes of achievement and satisfaction after the fact.

City life means panting as you chase after certain desires and unnecessary, yet necessary, luxuries. When we see these social sicknesses spread throughout the city, and laws passed to combat them, we are not surprised. We do not believe that they will end, and that we will gain victory over them, for the nature of city life is thus, and these sicknesses are inevitable. The city is dizziness and nausea, madness and loss, fear of insanity, fear of confronting urban life and its urban problems. It means fleeing from these things, trying to ignore them, compensating for moral and social emptiness, and the inability to satisfy these urban desires. Entertainment becomes a means to escape life, while drunkenness, madness, and suicide are possible ways of treating the diseases of urban life. Sometimes, and for some people, in fact a large percentage of them, urban life, with its aimlessness, superficiality, and lack of responsibility, is considered a treatment in and of itself.

Leave this hell on earth, run quickly away. In complete happiness, go to the village and the countryside, where physical labour has meaning, necessity, usefulness, and is a pleasure besides. There, life is social, and human; families and tribes are close. There is stability and belief. Everyone loves one another, and everyone lives on his own farm, or has livestock, or works in the village's service sector. Deviation is unacceptable, because the people in the village know one another, unlike those in the city. There, deviants know that they are not known by others; thus, a liar in the city is able to lie, without his lie requiring him, his family, or his tribe to answer questioning by society. A city dweller has no name, nickname, or title; his name is his apartment number. His nickname is his telephone number, and his title is his street or neighbourhood. These he changes from time to time. Thus, who he is now is not who he is afterwards.

How beautiful the village and countryside are! Clean air, the horizon before you, *the heavens without pillars thou canst behold,*[3] with their divine lanterns above. The conscience is healthy; moral example is the basis of moral action, and not fear of the police, the law, prison, or fines. There is liberation from all of these imposed restrictions and terrible necessities. There are no whistles sounding in the ears of those wanted, or not wanted. There are no one-way streets, no pushing others out of the way, no standing in line, no waiting, no looking at your watch. The village and countryside, the wide sky, joyfulness, the lord's dominion makes life peaceful and relaxing. It has none of the city's oppressiveness or crowds. The moon has a meaning, and there is pleasure

3.   Quran, Sura 13, verse 2.

gained by looking at the sky. You can see the horizon, as well as the sunrise, sunset, dawn, and dusk. Look at the beautiful picture the Quran draws for us of the village and countryside: *It needs not therefore that I swear by the sunset redness, and by the night and its gatherings and by the moon when at her full.*[4] The city has no moon or sun, no dawn or dusk. Its night is mixed with its day; there is no separation between them. There is no sign of nature. We see only artificial creation and ornamentation, we feel disturbances and annoyances, we live meaninglessly and marginally. We look down beneath our feet, read posters, watch for signs, get caught up out of necessity in trivialities, or else lose our very lives. Any looking or noticing other than these petty affairs puts you outside the context of city life, and could cost you your life, or urban freedom.

The Quran says: *By the sun and his noonday brightness; by the moon when she followeth him; by the day when it revealeth his glory; by the night when it enshroudest him; by the heaven and Him who built it.*[5] This beautiful verse is literally present in the

4.   Quran, Sura 84, verses 15-18.
5.   Quran, Sura 91, verses 1-6. In Arabic, the sun is a masculine noun, while the moon is feminine.

village and countryside. As well as *By the noon-day brightness; and by the night when it darkeneth.*[6] And when the dawn is invoked, we must remember that the dawn is seen only in the village and countryside. What dawn is there in a city, electrified day and night? Who sees the sky and the constellations of the zodiac? Upon the ground there are signs for those who believe. But what ground in the city? Busy sidewalks, crowded streets, bottlenecks, alleys, choke-points, limited vision. What signs can be seen in the streets of a city? What contemplation can take place in the crowdedness of the city? There is no time in the city, no night and no day. What about the night and all that it enshroudest,[7] the dark of night,[8] the dawn,[9] and the afterglow of sunset?[10]

---

6.   Quran, Sura 93, verses 1-2.
7.   Implicit reference to Quran, Sura 84, verse 17.
8.   Implicit reference to Quran, Sura 17, verse 78.
9.   Implicit reference to Quran, Sura 89, verse 1.
10. Implicit reference to Quran, Sura 84, verse 16.

The Earth

You can leave everything, except the earth. The earth is the only thing you cannot do without. If you destroy other things, you might not lose out, but beware of destroying the earth, because you will then lose everything! The source of biological life, at which human life stands at the top, is food. The earth is the container for this nourishment, which comes in different types... solid, fluid, gaseous. The earth is its container, so do not break the only container we have, for which there is no substitute. If you destroy agricultural land, for example, it is as if you are destroying the only vessel containing your food, without which you will not be able to consume it. If you destroy agricultural land, it is as if you are destroying the only vessel containing your drink, for which there is no other receptacle, so how will you be able to consume it! The earth is the lung through which you breathe, so if you destroy it, you will have no way to breathe. If the rain falls down upon you without having land, you will not benefit at all. Therefore, the sky has no value for us without our having land.

If oxygen is found somewhere in outer space, what is the benefit if there is no earth! All of history's conflicts throughout the ages have been led by man against man, or against nature, have been about land. Land has been the crux of the conflict. Even space has been used for the sake of land. Truly, the earth is your mother; she gave birth to you from her insides. She is the one who nursed you and fed you. Do not be disobedient to your mother—and do not shear her hair, cut off her limbs, rip her flesh, or wound her body. You must only trim her nails, make her body clean of dirt or filth. Give her medicine to cure any disease. Do not place great weights above her breast, weights of mud or stone above her ribs. Respect her, and remember that if you are too harsh with her, you will not find another. Sweep the accumulated iron, mud, and stone from her back. Relieve her of the burdens that others have placed on her unfairly. Revere the cradle in which you grew up, the lap in which you lay. Do not destroy your final resting-place, your place of refuge, or *you are the losers*[11] and you *shall truly regret it.*[12]

Land remains land only if we preserve its bounty. Land that is bountiful is truly useful land—guard it well. If we lay tile or pave it, build upon it, we will have killed it, and it will no longer give us its bounty. It will then become merely tile or asphalt, concrete or marble. And these things do not give us anything. They do not grow plants or give us water; they are useful neither to man nor animal. The earth will then have died. Do not kill the earth—do not kill your very life. The earth is water and nourishment, and the dead land that has been covered by buildings and construction does not give this water and nourishment. Thus, there is no life

11. Implicit reference to many verses; especially Sura 5, verse 30; Sura 2, verse 27; Sura 103, verse 2.
12. As in to become "repentant"; Quran, Sura 5, verse 31.

upon a dead earth. What kind of people are they who kill the earth and bury it alive! Upon what kind of land will their life depend afterwards! Where will they live, and where will they obtain their food and drink! The earth is something for which there is no alternative, so *whither then are you going!*[13] In heaven there are trees, and not roads, sidewalks, public squares or buildings. Ruining the earth is its misuse, its transformation into something other than land good for producing water and food. Thus, those who turn agricultural land into land that cannot grow anything are the ones *who spoil this land.*[14]

13. Quran, Sura 81, verse 26.
14. Quran, Sura 18, verse 94.

The Suicide
of the Astronaut

After man had travelled in outer space so much that he had become overcome by dizziness, after government budgets could no longer support expensive space programs, after man landed on the moon and found nothing, after the two astronauts exposed the wild speculations of scientists concerning the existence of seas and oceans on the moon's surface and the arrogant "Great Powers" competed over owning and naming them, almost coming into conflict over dividing the moon's wealth—especially marine resources—and after approaching the members of the solar system, taking their pictures and despairing of ever finding or being able to sustain life, man returned to the earth, dizzy, nauseous, and fearing doom. In fact, it was simply the case that the earth is the only known land, unique, a source of life. Life means water and food; the earth is the only place that provides us with these. The only true needs are bread, dates, milk, meat, and water. The only air necessary for life is that which surrounds the earth. And so, man returned to the earth from his adventure in outer space.

The astronaut removed his space suit and donned an ordinary one, so that he could resume his life upon the ground, having ended his mission in space. He began to look for earth-based work. He entered a carpenter's shop, but could not handle such simple tasks, since they were outside his area of specialization. The same went for his efforts at turnery, iron working, construction, and plumbing. He tried painting and white-washing as well, but had not studied drawing, or music, or knitting, since these were quite unconnected to his field of specialization. He left the industrial city *scorned, a banished one,*[15] and went to the countryside. He began to look for agricultural work, so that he could support himself and his family. A peasant asked him, "Do you know anything about tilling the good earth, son?" By asking this question, he was in fact asking if the astronaut liked farming.

The astronaut replied, "The earth's attraction decreases the higher we go, and our weight becomes gradually less until we reach the point of weightlessness. Then, we have freed ourselves of the earth's gravity, and eventually reach the gravitation of another planet, and our weight increases... and so forth and so on... I hope that I have answered your question."

The peasant looked as though he did not understand, as if he required further explanation. The astronaut went on, providing additional information, in the hope that he would gain employment on the land from the simple peasant.

"The earth's size is about 1,320 times less of that of Jupiter, while 12 earth-years equal one

15. Or, "rejected," a reference to Quran, Sura 7, verse 18.

year on Jupiter. The red spot of Jupiter is big enough to contain the earth at its centre, while Saturn is 744 times bigger than Earth. Even so, Earth's mass is only 95 times less than that of Saturn. The earth's diameter is about 50 times greater than the moon's, while its size is about 80 times greater. The earth's gravity is six times greater than the moon's. The earth is about 150 million kilometres distant from the sun, whose light takes eight minutes to reach us, travelling at a speed of 300,000 kilometres a minute. The earth's size is about 1,303,800 times less than the sun, while its mass is about 332,958 times less. Its density is approximately 30 times less than the sun's while the earth is the third most distant body from the sun. Mercury is the closest planet, followed by Venus, and then the earth. Venus is about 42 million kilometres from the earth, while the earth is about 400,000 kilometres from the moon. If you went by car, travelling 100 kilometres per hour, you would reach the moon in 146 days. If you did not have a car, and went by foot, you would arrive in eight years and 100 days. I think that answers your question. As you can see, I have complete knowledge about the earth."

When he said "earth," the peasant awoke

and closed his mouth, which had been open throughout the astronaut's journey from planet to planet, which began upon the earth and finally returned there. The peasant had understood nothing. In fact, he had become dizzy; he felt as if he had returned from a trip into space, throughout the entire solar system, but without any result for his farm. The distance that concerned him was that between one tree and another, and not between the earth and Jupiter. The weight that concerned him was the produce from his farm, and not of Mercury. Perhaps he felt sorry for the poor astronaut, and left him. The astronaut then committed suicide, after he gave up on being able to find work on the ground that could sustain him.

Escape to Hell

How cruel people can be when they rise up together, a crushing flood that has no mercy for anything in its path. Such a collectivity neither hears one's cry for help nor offers aid to anyone in need. Instead, it pushes one aside, heedlessly. The tyranny of an individual is the easiest kind of tyranny, since in the end, it is an individual that we are talking about. The group can get rid of him when it wishes; the individual may be removed by another individual, who himself may be worthless and unimportant. But the tyranny of the masses is the harshest type of tyranny, for who can stand against a crushing current, against a blind overwhelming force?

I love the freedom of the masses, as they move freely, with no master above them. They have broken their chains, singing and rejoicing following their pain and tribulation. Yet how I fear them! I love the masses as I love my father, yet fear them in the same way. In a bedouin society, with its lack of government, who can prevent a father from punishing one of his children? It is true that they love him, but they fear him at the same time. In the same way, I both love and fear the masses, as I love and fear my father.

The masses can be so compassionate when they are happy, carrying their sons upon their shoulders. In this way they carried Hannibal, Barclay, Savonarola, Danton, Robespierre, Mussolini, and Nixon, yet how harsh they can be when they become angry. They conspired against Hannibal and poisoned him, burnt Savonarola at the stake, brought their hero Danton to the guillotine. Robespierre was destroyed by his beloved fiancee, while the masses dragged Mussolini's corpse through the streets, and spat in

Nixon's face as he departed the White House for good, having applauded his entrance years before.

What terror! Who can address the unfeeling self and make it feel? Who can speak to a collective intelligence, embodied in no single individual? Who can hold the hand of the millions? Who can hear a million words from a million mouths at the same time? Within this all-encompassing uproar, who can be understood? Who blames whom?

With this social conflagration burning at your back, a society that loves you yet will never show you mercy, people who know what they want from this individual but pay no attention to his needs, they know what they are entitled to from you but have no care for their duty toward you...

Within this mass of people, who poisoned Hannibal, burnt Savonarola, and smashed Robespierre, who loved you but failed to reserve a seat for you at the cinema, or even a table in a cafe, who love you without expressing this in any simple way...

This is what the masses have done and continue to do to such people. So, what can I—a poor bedouin—hope for in a modern city of insanity? People snap at me whenever they see me: build us a better house! Get us a better telephone line! Build us a road upon the sea! Make a public park for us! Catch oceans of fish for us! Write down a magic spell to protect us! Officiate at our wedding! Kill this dog, and buy us a cat! A poor, lost bedouin, without even a birth certificate, with his staff upon his shoulder. A bedouin, who will not stop for a red light, nor be afraid when a policeman takes hold of him.

He eats without washing his hands, kicks anything out of his path, even if it goes through the nearest storefront, hits an old biddy in the face, or breaks the window of a beautiful white house. He does not know the taste of alcohol, or even Pepsi or any kind of soda. He would look for a camel in the middle of Sahat al-Shuhada, or a horse in Sahat al-Khadra, or would drive his sheep through Maidan al-Shajara.[16]

I feel that the masses, who would not even

16. Public squares in Libya, i.e., the sentence refers to a bumpkin looking for animals in urban places.

show mercy to their saviour, follow me around, burning me with their gaze. Even when they are applauding me, it feels like they are pricking me. I am an illiterate bedouin, who does not even know about painting houses or sewage systems. I drink rain water or well water using my hands, filtering out the tadpoles with my cloak. I do not know how to swim, whether on my stomach or on my back. I do not know what money looks like. Yet everyone I come across asks me for these things. In reality, I do not possess them; I took them from thieves, from the mouths of mice, from between the fangs of dogs. I distributed wealth among the people of the city as a benefactor come from the desert; as a liberator of fetters and chains. What has been stolen—and one of the thieves was a comrade of the cave-dwellers and the rats—requires a long time to take, the effort of more than a single individual. Yet, the mad people of the city constantly ask me for these things. I felt that I was the only one who did not own anything, so, unlike them, I did not ask for the services of a plumber, barber, etc. Since I had not requested anything, my situation became quite distinguished, or rather unnatural. Thus, I was and still am exposed to all of these requests and bother, although I must admit that I am partly responsible for this.

I wronged myself, when I stole Moses' staff, and with it struck the desert, as a spring of water burst forth.[17] As I said, I have no knowledge of sewage systems, plumbing, or narrow water lines, but had hoped that this spring would relieve me of answering all of those requests. Even my standing up to the policeman caused a commotion throughout the city, leading to people hearing about me. Some of them applauded me, while others cursed, and the police wanted to get rid of me. The mother of the policeman with whom I had argued took a fancy to me. When I refused her advances, she began to cause problems for me. The police sicked their stupid dogs upon me, while it was I who had taught them how to fish and make their living, so that they would leave me in peace and allow me to make my living with my sheep.

I am a poor, simple person. I have no royal blood; I am a bedouin. I have no doctorate; I do not even like physicians, because they are called

17. Implicit reference to Quran, Sura 2, verse 60; Sura 26, verse 63; Sura 7, verse 160, as well as to Libya's Great Man-Made River desert irrigation program.

"doctor." They could not inoculate me against sensitivity—I am very sensitive, unlike city people, who have been vaccinated from the days of the Romans until the Turks, and most recently under the Amelicans. As you see, to your amusement, I do not say "Americans," but "Amelicans," with an "l." This is because I do not know the meaning of America, which was not discovered by Columbus, but by an Arab prince.

But America is very powerful, has its agents and its military bases in areas of influence. It has the right of veto when it concerns the interests of Israel. It recently acquired a house at the head of the Nile Delta, where the river splits into the Rosetta and Damietta, and a buffalo farm surrounds the house... it is Amelica, as Hajj Mujahid says; he is the son of my aunt Azza, daughter of my grandmother Ghanima, who is the sister of Countess Maria.

On the whole, I did myself a disservice by coming to the city of my own free will, and this is no place to mention the reasons why. In any case, I may consider it a challenge, no more. Therefore, please leave me in peace to tend my flock, which I left in the valley under my mother's care. But my mother is dead, and my older sister as well. I was told that I had other brothers and sisters, but that they were killed by "mosquitoes." Leave me in peace, then. Why do you pursue me, and point me out to your children? Even they, now, are harassing me, and following me, saying, "I swear it is him." Why do you not leave me in peace, or at least walk through your streets undisturbed? I am a human being, like you; I like the taste of fruit, but why do you prevent me from entering your markets? And by the way, why do you not provide me with a passport? But what good would that do me, since I am forbidden from travelling, whether as a tourist or a seeker of medical treatment. I can only go on official business; this is why I have decided to make my escape to hell.

I will now tell you the story of my experiences when I made that journey, that escape to hell. I will describe the road that leads there, describe hell itself for you, and tell you how I came back by the same way. It was truly an adventure, and one of the strangest true stories ever, and I swear to you that it is not fiction. In fact, I escaped twice to hell, fleeing from you only in order to save myself. Your very breath bothers me, invading and violating my privacy; it seeks to squeeze me dry, greedily devouring my essence, licking up my sweat and sucking in my breath. Then it pauses, to give me a short breathing-space before it attacks me again.

Your breath chases me like a rabid dog, its saliva dripping in the street of your modern city of insanity. When I flee, it continues to chase me, through cobwebs and esparto. So I decided to escape to hell, if only to save myself.

The path to hell is not what you might expect, or what some false prophets may have described to you, a result of their own sick imagination. I will describe it to you—I, who took this path myself twice. I was able to sleep and rest in hell, and I can tell you that those two nights were among the most beautiful nights I have ever spent in my life, those two nights in hell, all by myself. They were one thousand times better than living among you. You hound me and keep me from having peace and quiet, so I was forced to escape to hell.

The path to hell is covered with an unending natural carpet, which I walked along merrily and happily. When the carpet came to an end, I found the road covered with fine sand. I was surprised to see flocks of wild birds of the kinds that we are used to seeing, and even saw some domestic animals grazing and grooming themselves. But I was astonished when I saw slopes and low ground below me; I stopped, hesitantly, and then saw hell off in the distance, at the edge of the horizon. It was not red as fire or glowing like embers. I stopped, but not out of fear of coming closer and reaching it, for that is what I wanted, after all—it was my refuge for your pursuing me in your tripolitan[18] city. When I saw it on the horizon, I could have almost flown into the sky out of joy. I stopped to choose the shortest path to take. I chose the one dearest to its heart, and stopped to listen if I could hear sighing and moaning, but it was completely still, quiet as the mountains around it.

It was a strange and wondrous silence that surrounded hell, a solemn silence. I saw no flames, but only rising smoke. I went down the slope joyously, hurrying to arrive before sunset and find a warm hearth to sit by, before I was

18. Literally, trebled city or tri-polis, the Greek name of Tripoli.

surrounded by hell's guardians, who I suddenly noticed were pursuing me. They had with them the latest means of detection. Finally, I drew quite close to hell, and was able to behold it from up close. I can now describe it to you, and tell you what I saw. I can answer any question you might have about it.

First of all, hell has wild, dark mountainsides, covered by fog. There is volcanic stone which has been burnt black since time immemorial. What is truly strange is that I found wild animals on their way to hell before me, also making their escape from you, for hell meant life to them, while life among you meant death. Everything then disappeared around me, except for my own existence, which I felt more strongly than at any previous time. The mountains shrank, the trees dried up, the animals bolted and melted into the jungles of hell, seeking refuge and fleeing mankind. Even the sun became obscured by hell, and began to disappear. Nothing remained clear except hell, and the most distinct part of it was its heart. I headed toward it, with practically no difficulty.

I began to melt within myself, as my self

also began to melt within me. Each of us protected the other and we became one for the first time. Not because my self was not a part of me before, but because the hell on earth never gave me the time to spend time with my self, contemplate it, and commune with it. For we—I mean me and myself—were like dangerous criminals in your city, subjected to searches and surveillance. Even after our innocence was proven, and our identity became known, we were placed in prison, guarded closely. Your purpose was always to prevent me and myself from coming together, so that you could sleep easily and contentedly. How beautiful hell is compared to your city! Why did you bring me back? I want to return to hell, and live in it. I would travel there without any passport, just give me myself so that I may go. The self that I discovered had been disfigured by you, as you tried to corrupt its innocence.

You tried to prevent me and myself from coming together, but by escaping to hell, I regained myself from you. I do not desire anything from you. You can have your trash; I left my golden helmet for you in Cairo—that venerable helmet that I took from the guardian after I had heard and read so much about it. I read that Aladdin's magic ring is made from its gold, and that whoever wore the ring would immediately become sultan, and could sit majestically upon a throne... kings and, presidents and princes would be forced to give way before him. He could bring the little Muaytiga[19] back to life, as well as all of the martyrs, from Omar Mukhtar, Saadun, Abdel Salam Abu Meniar, al-Jalit,[20] and all of those unknown soldiers.

Whoever wore the ring would receive four billion dinars, more or less, with which he could do what he wished. In general, he would obtain the genie's ring, which would get him whatever he wanted. It would gain him weapons, from rifles to intercontinental missiles. He could wish for a Mirage, to do with it what he wanted, let alone a MIG or a Sukhoi bomber; you could have the Englishman of your choice locked up in prison, and Thatcher could do nothing about it.

At the same time, if you were to wear the

19. Killed in an American bombing raid.
20. Heroes of the resistance to the Italian invasion.

magic helmet you could lazily go to sleep, even if you saw a wolf about to attack a herd of sheep in front of your very eyes. You could go to sleep for a number of years with your eyes wide open, among the heaps of garbage; but I heard on the Voice of the Arabs[21] that you have been deprived of this possibility. I read about the steel—excuse me—magic helmet that Lucifer, who bore the number 0 + 1, once claimed possession of, saying that he was an angel, and that Churchill and Truman bore witness to this.

You believed this lie, and were taken in by this deception; *the end of their conduct was ruin*.[22] In the end, I felt sorry for you, and heard the Friday prayer in your mosques: "Our sorry condition is not hidden from You, and our helplessness is plain to You. We have no shelter but with You; to You we return."[23]

---

21. Egyptian radio, made famous during the era of Gamal Abdel Nasser.
22. Quran, Sura 65, verse 9.
23. Derived from a pilgrim's prayer.

The Blessed Herb and the Cursed Tree

Good news for the mentally disturbed, whether male or female. A herb has been discovered in the plain of Benghazi, and it is now sold at Hajj Hasan's shop. In a television interview I personally conducted with him, and which was seen by more than three million people, Hajj Hasan said that the herb was a cure for the mentally disturbed. As for those who have not yet become mentally disturbed, Hajj Hasan said nothing about them. But as soon as they should become so, the herb will serve as their medicine. So much for the herb for the mentally disturbed. As for other diseases, Hajj Hasan has the required medicines, other than the blessed herb, at his shop as well. There are in fact other kinds of herbs. There is one for sterility, in all its forms (as he himself confirmed), lack of fertility, low productivity, perhaps even intellectual barrenness. There is also anti-dizziness medicine. If you should feel light-headed or dizzy for any reason, for example... if you get dizzy after shopping for a shirt for your son that costs one dinar at the state-owned store, then finding it at a private store for 20 dinars, returning to the state-owned store to find it gone, then back to the private store only to find that its price had risen to 25 dinars while you were gone only for five minutes, then Hajj Hasan can assure you that he has the right medicine for you, made from plants growing in green pastures. Moreover, there is another medicine, discovered by our Hajj Hasan as well, which is made from a kind of cactus, growing abundantly within the walls of old cemeteries. People who take this medicine gain the patience of the dead, even if they should be exposed up close and personally to local or international problems. And this is the secret of these plants, which grow in graveyards.

At the least, in this store, there is a long list of plants which, according to Hajj Hasan, allow you to dispense with the usual forms of treatment and prevention, such as hesitantly going to private and public clinics and hospitals. If only God gave us the wisdom to visit this store and wait in line for hours, or days, or months in order to get these medicines, we would be well rewarded. Why should we not be patient enough to wait in line to buy these medicines? We have cut down trees on farms and turned them into buildings; we have slaughtered animals, and will slaughter them again on the next feast-day. Society pays for the education of our children, while we receive audio-visual media free of charge; all we have to do is sit and watch and listen and criticize as much as we want. They purchase cartoons so that they, instead of us, can entertain our children. It does not matter whether these cartoons may be harmful or western... who has made them, and what are the animating ideas behind them? The important thing is that we do not work or produce or spend our time taking care of our children; all of this is done by society for us.

He who does not work, does not produce,

but yet he eats. As for defence, this does not appear to be one of his responsibilities, although we have lied to ourselves, and said, "Defence of the nation is the responsibility of every citizen, man or woman." We work hard to avoid this sacred duty. We call for peace and love, and our motto is "Peace, God's mercy and blessings be upon you";[24] for the Israelis our motto is "peace, mercy and blessings"(for the Americans as well as for the NATO Pact and the Pact of David). They should treat us in the same way, or even better. Every day, we wait for the Israelis to say: "Peace be on Rabta, Tajura, Ras Lanouf, Jerusalem, Baghdad." Truly, what need have we of medicine factories in Rabta and Ras Lanouf as long as we have Hajj Hasan and all of his herbal medicines which cure diseases, even afflictions such as sterility, heart problems, or bad eyesight, dysentery, or dignity.

But the interview began to fade out when Hajj Hasan was explaining the effects of a particular, important herb. I heard him say that it works against dysentery or dignity, and perhaps even old age, because I believe that I heard him

24. *Salaamu Alaykum wa Rahmat Allah wa Barakatihi*—a common Arabic greeting.

say "works against growing old or growing vain," or something like that, with apparently some connection to senility.[25]

Therefore, we are in fact happy, because we have freed ourselves from everything. There are poor people, unlike us, who defend their countries with their lives, and bleed for these causes. They sweat and toil to produce, digging the ground with their fingers. Plant trees, cucumber, garlic.[26] Poor Israelis, living with their fingers on the trigger to maintain their occupation of Palestine. Poor Noriega, and Oriega. Poor "Mericans," who spend billions on arming outer space so that they can defend America.

We, however, must go forward with this herb for treating the mentally disturbed, as well as using artichokes. We must set foot on this path, without hesitation, without being frightened by howls of denial—we must not let anything stand in our way. With complete determination, we must begin our trek. We must

25. The Arabic for "growing old" (kibar, or "senility") and "growing vain" (kibriya, or "pride") are homonyms.
26. Implicit reference to Quran, Sura 2, verse 6.

cut down trees, because the World Company was charged by the people to import cans, even from the sky. Move on, now that you have been liberated and the power has become the people's, and no one else's. Onward, to eradicate agriculture and tear out its roots. Hurry to transform—not in a revolutionary way—but rather transform yourselves into merchants, pastry peddlers, and travelling salesmen. Teach your children how to make deals and get commissions, sell the choicest swamp land or property on other planets. You free men, my friends: whether in the middle of the day or night, you should continue to cut down trees and erase greenery on the face of the good earth. With your muscled arms, destroy the forests of Jabal al-Akhdar[27] and palm trees of your farms; over their corpses construct stores, beauty shops, candy shops, limestone quarries. What does a palm tree matter, since the world is making our sweets for us? We prefer dates without any thorns, oranges with no peels, olives with no trees. Cut down the trees, especially the cursed palm and olive tree.

In this way, we will become equal with the

27. In eastern Libya.

haughty, powerful nations. We will be safe from nuclear missiles; we will defeat backwardness, which has lasted for so long, and create progress.

Death

Is death male or female? God only knows. However, the pre-Islamic poet Tarafa Bin al-Abd considers it masculine, saying:

> I see death hover over the generous
> taking the hoarded treasures of their
> most unrelenting

The contemporary, but also pre-Islamic[28] poet, Nizar Qabbani, says that it appears to be

28. Qaddafi is accusing Qabbani of a lack of piety.

female, since it took his son Tawfiq. But why the question? What good does it do to determine whether death is male or female? Death, after all, is death. However, it is our duty to specify its sex, and find out whether it is male or female. If it is male, then we must combat it to the last breath, and if it female, then we should surrender to it in the end. In any case, the word death appears in many books, sometimes in a male sense and sometimes female.

From my experience and pains, I can confirm this. Death is male, and is always on the offensive; it is never in a defensive position, even if it has been defeated. It is fierce and bold, cunning and cowardly sometimes. Death attacks and is defeated; he is turned back forcefully at times, not always victorious as some people might think. How many face-to-face battles took place when death lost its strength, and retreated defeated? But despite the blows and the wounds he would receive when facing a tenacious opponent, he never once surrendered or fell prisoner. He never once went down in defeat, and this is his dangerous secret, his tremendous superiority, facing all of the elements that work against death.

Death is a truly incomparable combatant, with unlimited patience. He has complete self-confidence when facing an opponent, no matter how strong or victorious. No matter how many times death loses a battle, is wounded, or hears the victory celebrations by his short-sighted opponents, he does not lose hope that he cannot attack again. He is truly a determined adversary, who never gives up.

The power of death does not lie in his decisive blows, fatal stabs, or successful attacks, for he hits and misses, wins and loses, attacks and is defeated. Not all of his blows are perfectly aimed, nor are all of his battles won. Instead, his might lies in his hellish power to absorb and neutralize all of those spears and arrows that hit him, and in his evil appetite for sucking the blood from the wounds of his victims, transforming it into his fiery fighting energy, which inevitably leads to his opponent's defeat.

Death is deserving of victory because he is impartial, and seeks help from nobody. That would constitute a deficiency, and death has none of those. It would indicate that death was the lackey of someone else; in fact, death maneuvers and changes colour like a chameleon, and can do no one else's work. If he were to depend on some ally, he would become a hostage. A hostage is not free, a hostage is a doll, that can be thrown away after its being used in a game. If death were someone's lackey, or stooge, hostage, or doll, then his inevitable victory would certainly arouse suspicion. Death, as I have said, is not a hero of legend with high ideals, good social and tribal behaviour, and good family upbringing such that he behaves properly so that these attributes do not suffer. Death is a sly fox, a chameleon, capable of taking on different personalities and forms to suit his whim. He may appear as a knight on a white house, brandishing his weapon openly in the face of his opponent, or he may stab him in the back like a woman who is untrained at fighting. He may approach fearlessly, then suddenly fall to the ground and continue stealthily and deceptively.

Death has claimed so many victims as they were completely unaware of his presence, or sleeping peacefully. Other victims were taken as they laughed heartily, oblivious of him. Do not expect mercy or pity from death! He will not be pleasant with you, appreciate your circumstances, or respect your lives. He would tear an infant from its mother's breast, or snatch a fetus from its mother's womb. He might kidnap a bride or groom on the wedding night; he might attack parents and leave the children, or vice versa. As the yellowing books say about him, death is the terminator of pleasure, and the orphan-maker of girls and boys.

Therefore, do not show any mercy to death or expect any from him. It is a settled matter between us; he is our deadly enemy, and there can be no reconciliation, or hope of such a thing. Do not show him any mercy or let him see any dissension in your ranks. He will show you no mercy, no matter how weak you may be, or if you have surrendered. He is against the principle of reconciliation, and has no truck with peaceful coexistence. He cut down my brothers and sisters in the prime of their lives, and starved my family until they were forced to journey to his land. He drowned my brothers and sisters in a quagmire, poisoning them. Four boys and two girls. He entered into punishing battle with my brave father. He came to Qardabia during Miani's[29]

29. An Italian officer who participated in the campaign against Libya.

campaign, dressed as Italian and Eritrean soldiers so that he could kill my father, who had been in open struggle with him since the death of my brothers and sisters. My father had decided to take his revenge on death, and killed many of Colonel Miani's soldiers. Their clothes and bodies had been taken over by death in a camouflage maneuver, such that each one had become death itself.

My father was very bewildered as row upon row of martyrs fell, to his left and right without interruption. He thought that with every bullet, he was killing death, until he ran out of ammunition, and shouted, "Can you give me the ammunition so that for your sakes, I can do away with death?" A youth, lying prone in a nearby trench, said that he had a full belt to give. My father happily raced toward him, only to find upon reaching him that he was dead.

Thus, death can hear and see, but my father was as fierce a combatant as death. He took the young man's ammunition and continued to struggle against death, until he was overtaken by a deadly thirst. My father asked his uncle Khamis for some water so that he could carry on the fight. Khamis went to a water-carrying mule in the Italian lines, to help my father. But death, as usual, was faster, and fired a fatal shot at Khamis, hitting him above the eyebrow, which entered the brain and exploded it. Khamis fell. My father went mad and charged out of his trench, ready to fight in the open and challenging death to face-to-face combat. He said. "We are the children of Moses! If you are truly a man, come out and fight like one, and not a coward."

Death, however, did not answer this provocation, or even raise his hand or face to indicate his position. Instead, he answered with white-hot lead. And it was a group of brave young men who answered my father's call, calling out, "We are the Hajj's children... we are the Hajj's children." They stood up and faced death fearlessly. My father hurried to them to join their attack, but again, death was faster. He mowed them down before my father could get there. As the fight between death and my father became fiercer, his comrades asked him not to come closer, so that death would not take them as it did Khamis, the Hajj's sons, al-Atrash, al-Sohbi, Muhammad Bin Faraj,[30] and the others. From

30.   Libyans who fought against Italian occupation.

morning till night, my father fought against
death, until finally death's power began to recede,
and his determination became weakened. Death
decided to flee, and conserve his strength for
another day. He had put nine bullets in my
father's clothes and body, but could not finish
him off.

As I told you, death is sometimes defeated
and runs away, but never feels shame or despair,
because his self-confidence his stronger. He is
certain that his final victory is greater than any
temporary defeat, or passing setbacks. The secret
is that he is the source of his power, and does not
depend on America!

Not more than three years later did death
re-take the initiative, with the hope of defeating
my father this time. A ferocious battle took place
between them, much worse than the one at
Qardabia. Using his typically deceptive ways,
death appeared disguised in the clothes and very
being of a royal Senussi soldier, who was fighting
on the side of the Italians in Sirte and Ejdabia. If
death was confident of victory this time, proud of
his superior forces and fire-power, my father was
even more defiant. Even if my father was less

confident and hopeful of victory, he was angrier and more enraged. Death laughed as he saw the Senussi soldiers crawling like locusts to occupy the area surrounding the Klaya pit near the salt mine, turning the colour of the sand from gold to black and white, depending on their uniforms. The area was filled with hundreds of soldiers from death's army. My father saw only a small number of his lion-like fighting men, in addition to some others. *A stern and calamitous day,*[31] with death fully prepared and my father armed only with his bravery.

Death led the hosts of pro-Italian Senussi soldiers, while my father had his band of noble, brave men. Since the position was a difficult one to defend and the prospect of help so dim, the battle so unequal, my father decided to do battle, throwing all caution to the wind. He openly announced his contempt of death and his army, and whatever might come to pass. My father dug no trenches nor fired from a prone position. His desperation and bravery became intermingled, and how awesome they were to behold! How hard it was to stay alive! Death's

31. Quran, Sura 76, verse 10.

blows were felling his comrades, but not touching him, just like at Qardabia. Abu Isba was hit in the heart; Qaddaf al-Damm, taking his last breath. The sun was falling to earth, as if it had been hit as well. In a little while darkness would cover everything, causing death to lose the opportunity.

Death swelled up, enraged at my father, whom he had challenged since the morning. He took aim at my father with a Moscov rifle, which the Czar of Russia had given him. Death aimed at the heart, but instead pierced my father's shoulder, inflicting a dangerous wound. As I told you, not all of death's blows find their mark, and not all of them are fatal. He hits and misses, and wins and loses. However, he weakened my father so that he could not continue the fight, and caused him partial, permanent paralysis, but he did not lose his life on this day.

As I told you, death is not always brave, and does not always take the initiative. He is sometimes cowardly, stabbing his victim in the back, stinging him in the foot, melting away into the ground. Death, as I have told you, does not despair, so despite growing weary after encountering many heroes in battle, such as at al-Milh and Qardabia, where he failed to defeat my father, he appeared next in the guise of a striped snake. Death hid under a trunk of a thorny desert bush in a treeless valley, waiting to treacherously bite the heel of my father in the dead of the night.

This is frightening death, riding his black horse during a moment of intense anger, or his white horse when defiantly challenging: his opponent. Death, who unsheathed his sword in the face of great leaders without fear. Death, who disappears from sight and skulks toward his opponent from behind, approaches from above, from below. He bites and does not scab, he shrinks and disappears, aims at the heel instead of the neck. This is how frightful death, whose terror fills the sky, transformed itself in front of my father into an evil poisonous snake. My father's rough foot trod on it, but it managed to bite him, thinking that its stratagem had worked. After death had failed in open confrontation, it resorted to ruses; a daytime confrontation became a nighttime obfuscation. I would think that a desert snake biting a person alone in a distant valley, where no one could hear his cry for help, would mean certain death for that person. But death's haughty expectation of victory was such that he neglected the fact that a person's will can overcome death, and disappoint all expectations. The will to live can negate the effects of fatal poison, by simply using a strong brew of black tea without sugar. Several doses of this drink made my father vomit a number of times, after which he sprung to his feet, overcoming death, which had appeared victorious only moments before. My father mocked his opponent, crushing the head of the snake with his heel.

But death, as we all know from this story, does not die or despair, no matter how badly hurt or beaten he may be. My father killed that snake with his strong foot, which had been mighty and undefeated in battle or in crushing the heads of other snakes. Death, however, quickly fled from under my father's foot, and took refuge in another snake, lying on the road that my father took to return home. When he was reaching for a match stick to light a fire, that second snake bit his hand and emptied into it a full dose of its fatal venom. On this occasion my father had no tea and the place was not remote and isolated, where my father's death would be catastrophe.

Therefore, death considered it was to his advantage that there lacked the atmosphere of challenge, which would bring out the best in my father. Death thought that my father would not have the spirit to challenge him, since this time there were people around and my father's having to ask them for help and rely on them would deprive him of his fighting spirit. Thus, death thought that his stubborn opponent would not escape from him this time. However, death had stupidly forgotten that repeated snake bites had immunized my father from their effect. This second bite by death had only a little effect, and though painful, it was not fatal.

As my father lived on, death retained its ambition; as my father remained stubborn, death continued to try to fell him.

So far, in telling this dramatic story, we can say that death is definitely male in all but these final situations, in which it turns out to be female. The matter is a confusing one, since even when death turned into a female snake, she had to be fought against as if she were male. A poisonous snake is a fierce enemy, and as an enemy she must be fought against in this way, just as if she were an Eritrean or Italian soldier in the battle of Qardabia. Since we began our story by dealing with the issue of whether death is male or female; if it is male, then we must combat it to the last breath, and if it female, then we should surrender to it in the end.

So far in this story, my father fought back and did not surrender, and so we can consider death male. But recently, I became convinced that death is female, because my father finally surrendered to her on May 8, 1985, raising not an arm to resist her. For the first time, I saw him surrender, and in fact he had even refused efforts at intervening between him and death, defending it in a way, which indicates that it is female, or female in the ancient way that the Quran talks about; *And they make the angels who are the servants of God of Mercy, females.*[32] He was defending it against any interference, while he could have resisted. He gave in to death peacefully, as if it was nothing to be frightened of, and had never been that fully armed fighter whose appearance made men like my father offer resistance.

32.   Quran, Sura 43, verse 18.

The drums of death, which got louder, are nothing more than a hypnotizing song of Um Kalthoum.[33] The nearer that death approached, the drumbeats became heavier and more annoying. My father relaxed in his bed, smiling as innocently as a baby in a cradle. He became more relaxed and content, until it seemed to us that the noisy accompaniment of death's chariot, which would frighten healthy people, was to the sick like a hypnotizing song by a famous Egyptian singer.

I thought that chemical anaesthetics were not needed to treat patients, but that a long Egyptian song would do. The doctor objected to this, and rejected any interference in his field. He assured me that my thoughts and conclusions were erroneous and contained not a grain of truth, and could under no conditions be relied upon. I became embarrassed about my lack of knowledge of anaesthesiology, but saved the doctor the embarrassment of continuing as I continued for him.

I added, speaking for him, of course, that I

33.   Egyptian female singer.

was completely ignorant of this science, and had mixed up anaesthetizing the sick and hypnotizing the well. That I had exaggerated the power of Egyptian songs, thinking that they could affect the sick. Of course, they only affect people who are well, and have done so since 1948 quite effectively. They were used on more than 100 million Arabs, and proved to be an amazing success. Unfortunately, contrary to what I had expected, it became necessary to use chemicals for treating patients and performing operations, since the songs seemed to have no effect on them. In fact, doctors recommend that sick people not listen to these songs, because they might result in complications or nausea. People in good health, however, and also those with mental problems, are advised to listen to these songs, if they would like to enter an artificial type of coma or non-chemically induced anaesthesia. Doctors have confirmed that there are no side-effects in these cases. If there were such complications, of course, they would affect these people's productivity and well being, but as far as their bodies are concerned, there is nothing to worry about. When I noted that this might affect the mind and spirit, the doctor replied casually, "The spirit, the mind, temperament, and such things are intangible and do not concern the surgeon."

In general, as my father became weaker and weaker, we became tenser and tenser and filled with pain and dread. At times we would cry, while he would smile, at peace within his coma. Who knows if it was death with which he fought at Qardabia, Talla, and al-Milh. Was it death who was the poisonous snake which accosted him in the empty desert and on other occasions? Was death his bitter, recalcitrant enemy, whose arrogance caused his opponent to become more reckless? I do not think it was him, because if it were, there would have been no one to rival him in the art of camouflage and deception. But this time, my father did not fight back, as he had done all his life, when he was always victorious, despite the many narrow chances. Thus, death is female, and in this case, one must surrender until the last breath, which is what my father did.

The result, then, is that death may fail in battle most of the time, coming from under a cloud with black banners waving in the heart of the storm. In this case, death believes he is riding the favourite horse in the race, when in fact he is riding the horse of vanity. In this way, he causes his opponent to experience extreme anger and the loss of self-control, which leads to his defeat. In this way, death appears as a very brave man who must be resisted until the end, and most of the time successfully. But there are other, dangerous times when death wins easily, and changes from masculine to feminine. And you must surrender to a female until the last breath, as we said at the beginning of this story. Surrender never brings victory; when death changes his tactics, he expects his opponent to surrender when he appears as a woman, and thus achieves victory without any resistance.

Thus, death will always attain its goal in the end, no matter how long the struggle, and will never show mercy to his opponent, even if he surrenders, shows weakness, or shows himself to be like Sadat![34]

You must resist death all your lives, if you wish them to be long, just as my father never surrendered to death, and fought him without fear until he reached the age of 100. This was

34. For signing the peace treaty with Israel.

despite death's wishes, since he wanted to end his life at the age of 10. The correct action is confrontation, because fleeing abroad will not save you from death. The Quran says: *Wherever ye be, death will overtake you-although ye be in lofty towers!*[35] But if death himself weakens, and becomes a non-Libyan[36] or non-Latin female, coming forward peacefully and without being armed, entering quietly and enticingly until we feel her in every part of our bodies, making us enraptured with her charms, begins to tickle us until we laugh mirthfully, then it would not be manly to resist her and fight—it would be our duty to surrender to her until the last breath... and this is what happened.

35. Quran, Sura 4, verse 80.
36. Literally, a "non-jamahariyya female," "jamahariyya," or "state of the masses," is an official part of the name of the Libyan state.

Jacob's Cursed Family and the Blessed Caravan

Who of us has not heard of the family of Jacob? Or rather, who of us does not hold this family in high regard? Why not, since the members of this family, in all the world, are quite proud of being Jacob's descendants, and the descendants of the prophet Joseph, the keeper of the granaries' wealth in ancient Egypt. How could anyone ignore Joseph and his true prophecies? All of us know this; the entire world knows. He could divine the future, a trusted and trustworthy[37] interpreter of dreams, chosen by God, who taught him the *interpretation of dark stories*.[38] He was so good-looking that the wife of Aziz of Egypt *conceived a passion for him, but rent his shirt behind,* proving that she was a liar. He was desired by the ladies of the city, who slashed their hands, and said, *God keep us! This is no man! This is no other than a noble angel!*[39] He almost returned their desires, but then saw in a vision the future of Egypt, how it would be overtaken by lean years following years of plenty; years of drought after years of prosperity.

Therefore, the family of Jacob have a right to be proud of themselves, since it is a great and blessed family. Its forefather was the *grieving Jacob,*[40] and his son was Joseph. Do they not deserve our honour and reverence? That a path at an airport be opened for them? That they receive special treatment at weddings and other social occasions, and even at conferences, that they be singled out and held in estimation for being

37. See Quran, Sura 12, verses 54-55.
38. Quran, Sura 12, verse 6.
39. Quran, Sura 12, verses 23, 25, 31.
40. See Quran, Sura 12, verse 84.

Joseph's brothers? The family has truly been gloried by God!

This is what we knew about the family of Joseph, enough to make us honour and esteem its members. However... we should also know that the family was cursed, and not covered in glory, or blessed. A false halo of holiness was created for it; its glory was certainly undeserved.

The cursed family of Jacob, even though Isaac was its grandfather and Joseph its son, was one of the basest and most impious and hypocritical of families, truly deserving of contempt and scorn. Did they not claim that they had guarded Joseph from the wolves, hoping for his safety? Did their father not say to them, *I fear lest while ye are heedless of him the wolf devour him? And did they not reply, Surely if the wolf devour him, and we so many, we must in that case be weak indeed?*[41]

The cursed family of Jacob came up with a devious plan for one of its own. As its members conspired against Joseph, they said, *Slay Joseph or*

41. Quran, Sura 12, verses 13-14.

drive him to some other land! They argued among themselves over the best way to carry out their plan, and betray their father, Jacob. One of them said, *Slay not Joseph, but cast him down to the bottom of the well.* But Joseph knew of this, while they did not, as they *brought his shirt with false blood upon it.*[42]

The cursed family of Joseph, lying and deceitful, treacherous. They stripped him of his clothes, and stained them with false blood, took him away, and threw him down a well. They did all of this, while Joseph heard and saw, but did not scream in their faces and say to them, "Traitors... filth... How can you be my brethren?"

Joseph was extremely patient, as God revealed to him that *Thou wilt yet tell them of this their deed, when they shall not know thee.*[43] Joseph was the most innocent of innocence with them, smiling at them and joking with them, while they lowered him into the well. He knew what they were doing, and knew that it would not succeed. But he did not say, "You are being treacherous and deceitful to your father." He did not say,

42. Quran, Sura 12, verses 9, 10, 15, 18.
43. Quran, Sura 12, verse 15.

"One day I will tell you of this deed and your races will turn black with shame, for you are guilty and will be scorned and hated by everyone."

Meanwhile, they merely looked at him and smiled, all the while plotting against him and carrying out their deceitful plan. *They plotted, and God plotted: But of those who plot is God the best.*[44]

The cursed family of Jacob, and the blessed caravan. Yes, it was the caravan which rescued Joseph from the depths of the well, after his brothers had left him. The caravan lowered its bucket and when they brought it back up, they found Joseph in it. It was the blessed caravan which saved him, and he received good treatment in the city.

The cursed family of Jacob, and the blessed caravan. After this shameful scandal, who among us would honour the family of Joseph, or trust them with him?

However, Joseph's brothers did not kill

44. Quran, Sura 3, verse 44.

him, although they could have, seeing as how they were entrusted with his care. Truly, they did not kill him, perhaps because they fell out with one another about how to go about it, as it says in the Quran, or because they did not have the courage to go through with it. Or, because they were his brothers, they could not have borne seeing his actual blood spilled, so they preferred that he die slowly at the bottom of the well. Or, perhaps again because they were his brothers, they could not have allowed him to be killed, in any manner, so they allowed his fate to be decided by the caravan. They appeared to know that it would not leave him to die. *Slay not Joseph, but cast him down to the bottom of the well: if ye do so, some wayfarers will take him up.*[45] And it is most likely that fear of their father and others was the true reason for their action.

The cursed family of Jacob, and the blessed caravan. We were deceived when we honoured them, because Joseph was their son. We were dazzled by the procession of sun, moon, and planets around Joseph, and said, Verily I beheld eleven stars and the sun and the moon. We preferred, or were forced, to look on from a

45. Quran, Sura 12, verse 10.

distance, with open-mouthed amazement. If we closed our mouths, we would clap warmly and say, *Verily I beheld eleven stars and the sun and the moon—beheld them make obeisance to me.*[46]

Now in Joseph and his brethren are signs for the enquirers.[47] But what if this family were exposed? What if Joseph's brothers planned this abominable treachery which made people recoil in sheer terror? The skies were about to burst, the earth split asunder, the mountains tumbled, while a shudder of violent revulsion possessed those who heard it. Thus, the family of Jacob were responsible for a most monstrous act. But what if they had retained their honour among people, and Joseph's brothers had lived to serve him as apostles, guarding him and caring for him and listening to what he had to say?

Did God not forgive them in the end? *He took his parents to him and said, "Enter ye Egypt, if God will, secure."* He raised his parents on a throne, while they fell prostrate. *Then said he, "O my father, this is the meaning of my dream of old. My Lord hath now made it true, and he hath surely*

46. Quran, Sura 12, verse 4.
47. Quran, Sura 12, verse 7.

been gracious to me, since he took me forth from the
prison, and hath brought you up out of the desert."[48]

However, Jacob's family did do a good
thing, because, even without this ugly scandal, or
scandalous ugliness, Jacob's family is ugly and
scandalous, even though we used to think of
them as a great family. This is not because they
had a glorious history in the past, great wealth, or
water or houses and a "high ceiling." On the
contrary; the family's origins were not well
known, they were low bred, humble, and
subservient, living in the desert, as the Quran
mentions. They were a family of shepherds; the
greatest victory for one of Joseph's brothers
would have been to kill a wolf or a fox. They
could have never dreamed of victories over
reactionary imperialism. This universal glory
would never have entered the head of one of
Jacob's family. No one dreamt of the glory of the
treasures of Egypt except Joseph, who could see
the future and specialised in interpreting visions.
If not for this event, what would have happened
to the family of Jacob, or to the whole world?
People could have carried them on their
shoulders out of reverence. Had they not

48. Quran, Sura 12, verse 100.

begotten Joseph? How could they have taken
other than the common path that the multitude
takes; how could this have happened to Jacob's
family, which brought forth Joseph, who received
revelation from God, who made him a prophet,
guardian of the treasury of the land, interpreter of
dreams, desired by women?

Thank God, who has revealed the family of
Jacob to us in the Quran; they were not the
guardians of Joseph, but were dealing with them
calmly, he was attempting to gain glory for them
while they were plotting to throw him down the
well.

The family of Jacob were both wicked and
foolish. Joseph was building for them a house of
glory, while they were tearing it down with their
own hands.

However, we must be as fair as we can to
the family of Jacob, if there is someone to whom
we can be fair. Yes, it appears that there are the
oldest and the youngest, who was their half
brother, as the Quran says. The oldest of them
was the one who said to those treacherous ones
that Joseph should not be killed, but thrown

down the well, to be rescued by passing travellers. As for their half-brother, the youngest of them, he was on the side of Joseph, and was hated by the members of that cursed family. They wanted to get rid of him as well and betray him as they had betrayed Joseph. They left him as a hostage in Egypt, when they went to beg Joseph for grain, Joseph whom they did not recognize.

The cursed family of Jacob and the blessed caravan.[49]

---

49. A reference to Quran, Sura 86, verse 17.

Stop Fasting When You See the New Moon

The prophet Muhammad said, "Begin fasting when you see the new moon, and end your fasting when you see the new moon again. If it is overcast, continue your fasting for thirty days." This is the Islamic tradition followed by Muslims in this matter. However, following this tradition every year gets Muslims into difficulties concerning the beginning and end of the month of Ramadan, as well as the Hajj,[50] except for this year, and we will see if this difficulty gets resolved

50. The pilgrimage to Mecca.

this year. The ability to see the new moon varies
from one region to another, and even one
continent to another, since Islam has spread
worldwide and local ways of observing these
things are no longer adequate. Seeing the new
moon in the Arabian peninsula, in Mecca and
Medina, was probably what was meant at the time,
since means of communication were practically
non-existent. One could not have expected that
news from Yemen about seeing the new moon
would arrive in Mecca and Medina, since the
journey would have taken more than one month.

Nowadays, the world has become
completely interconnected, at the speed of sound,
or 340 metres per second. It is very possible for
information about sighting the new moon to
spread quickly throughout the world today, but
the problem has not been solved by this
dangerous, scientific transformation. Rather, the
problem has become more complicated since we
know more about the world than we did before.
Consequently, disputes have become greater
between Muslim learned men and laymen, sultans
and common people. The Saudis do not want the
Hajj to fall on a Friday because of the great crowds
and the resulting problems, and they have every

right to be worried about this. And they would be even more justified should it be confirmed that the Hajj falling on a Friday leads to the death of a member of the royal family, God forbid. Thus, our brethren in Saudi Arabia are quite unenthusiastic about the Hajj falling on a Friday; let it be on a Saturday or a Sunday, rather than facing the risk of losing a prince... God forbid!

With all of these facts and new types of information and faster communication, we assumed that having a unified beginning and ending to the month of Ramadan, and thereby a unified Hajj, would become easier. However, it became clear to us that Friday in Indonesia is Thursday in Libya; in other words, it could be 30 Shaaban[51] in Libya, and the beginning of Ramadan in Indonesia or the Solomon Islands in the Pacific. If Indonesia were to telephone and announce that the new moon had been sighted, Libya would be in the month of Shaaban. Thus, sighting the new moon is limited to a certain region, and very limited, as each region should begin and end its fasting according to its own sightings. But the real difficulty lies elsewhere.

51. The month in the Islamic lunar calendar preceding Ramadan, the month of fasting.

Practically speaking, the beginning and ending of fasting do not create any problems, unlike the Hajj. If people began their journey of pilgrimage from every corner of the world,[52] having already set the dates for the rituals of circling the Kaaba, walking to Mount Arafat, and casting stones at the devil on the basis of the beginning of the lunar year, then each group of Muslims would be acting on the basis of different dates. Each group would have different days for the atonement at Arafat, the day of Sacrifice, and other Hajj rituals. This is an important spiritual and practical problem for our Saudi brethren.

However, this issue was settled only this year by General Nour[53] Schwarzkopf himself, may God's blessing be upon him. He had decided previously, from the first week of Ramadan, that the holiday would fall on Monday, April 15, 1991 of the Christian calendar. Thus, he also definitively decided that the Hajj would fall on a certain group of days, according to the western calendar. This was regardless of whether sighting was possible or not (I mean sighting the new moon, and not the

52. Or "every deep ravine"; Quran, Sura 27, verse 22.
53. A sarcastic use of the Arabic name Nour (light) for Norman.

general in question), or whether the month of Shaaban had 29 or 30 days, or whether Ramadan had 28 or 30 or 31 days. The matter was not open to discussion, and not subject to whether the new moon was sighted or not. The issue was not a matter of religious tradition or religious obligation. So said the prophet, and so said God. Schwarzkopf's decision could not be appealed; it involved the security of the American forces and their allies, the security of the entire Kingdom of Saudi Arabia, which includes the house of God and the tomb of the Prophet.

Ramadan, then, had to end at the latest on a Sunday, even if for security reasons, on April 14, 1991. For all Muslims, whether they began fasting on a Saturday, Sunday, or Monday, the 14th meant the 14th, even if it was overcast or they strained themselves trying to make out the new moon. And we can take it for granted that whether or not the new moon had arrived, the first day of Shawwal had to be April 15, 1991. Even if a new month for the Hajj had to be found, such as the months of Shawwal or Dhu al-Qada. If General Nour's timetable were rejected, Muslims could enjoy respect and sovereignty in matters of religion and choose any month they preferred. As Schwarzkopf himself said, this did not contradict the Quran. The Quran says, "The months of the Hajj are well known."[54] Thus, this means several months, and not just one. General Schwarzkopf decided this Islamic issue, which had plagued Muslims for many years, as it involved sighting the new moon. There is no need, Muslims, for you to trouble yourselves in looking for the new moon of the month Shawwal,[55] for the matter is decided. It was officially announced in the Kingdom of Saudi Arabia that Ramadan ended on a Sunday. Shawwal ended on Sunday, and the hell with you, your new moon, and your religious and non-religious courts of law. General Schwarzkopf had decided that all formalities for the pilgrimage in all parts of the world should be completed before the end of Ramadan. For this reason, he decided when Ramadan should end, because for the first time this action went along with arrangements for the Hajj.

The Hajj was of concern to General Schwarzkopf because the entry of hundreds of thousands of people from around the Islamic world to areas under his control was a very

54. Quran, Sura 2, verse 43.
55. The month following Ramadan.

dangerous matter. The Hajj, this year, was not like other years. This year, Mecca and Medina were under the protection of American forces, and according to what you already know yourselves, the Saudi government requested the protection of these forces when Iraq entered Kuwait and threatened to enter the holy places, to make them part of Iraq. This was a very dangerous affair, and might have involved these forces marching to the oil fields. Thus, it was the Saudi government's right to ask for this protection, since it is an independent country, with the right to decide what it wishes. It was in America's interest to approve this request and carry it out; were it not for the American forces, Mecca and Medina today might be under Iraqi control despite the positives and negatives of this. However, the protection provided by American forces prevented this, and we cannot blame General Schwarzkopf if he designated the end of Ramadan and the beginning of Shawwal, and when the rituals of Mount Arafat, sacrifice, and throwing pebbles at the devil should take place, and that the last day of Ramadan was the final day for registering for the Hajj.

Thus, we cannot leave the issue of when

Ramadan ends to the sighting of the new moon, because this conflicts with the security of troops responsible for protecting the Kingdom of Saudi Arabia. The general was forced to set April 14 as the end of Ramadan and April 15 as the beginning of Shawwal, etc., and the other rituals according to the western calendar. General Schwarzkopf ordered the pilgrims in the house of God that, in addition to the prohibitions against lewdness, wickedness, and dispute during the Hajj, there was an additional list of prohibitions, for which he, and not God, was responsible. The list prohibited a pilgrim from bringing with him any pictures, other than the one in his passport, and any book, including the Quran and other holy Islamic scripture. The general also forbade praying unless the prayers were those prepared by the general himself, and could be found at all hajj guides' offices.[56] This was to be followed strictly because freedom of expression, without fixed texts of prayers, could lead people to shout slogans against the American forces, or even the general himself, or the president, God forbid.

56. Guides to the hajj, who accompany Muslims and assist
    them in carrying out the rituals of the pilgrimage.

This might lead to demonstrations and other types of protest, which could affect security, for which the American forces were responsible. Mecca, after all, is an indivisible part of the Kingdom of Saudi Arabia, and Schwarzkopf was responsible for its protection. What is the problem with extending the month of Ramadan to 32 days, with the holiday falling on the third of Shawwal (instead of the first), or with accepting military orders concerning procedures for the Hajj?

Who was in the wrong? Certainly, it was the one who did not toe the line, and disobeyed orders. Why should you look to the sky and attempt to sight the moon? Instead, just say that the sky is overcast. In this way, you would be killing several birds with one stone. Most importantly, you would be following religious tradition, since it was overcast, and so Ramadan had to last 32 days. Moreover, you would be gaining holiness by fasting those additional two days, and who would oppose you on this, or call you an unbeliever? Your answer could be from the Quran: *And good shall it be for you to fast.*[57] You would be bowing your head submissively before God, as it is prescribed in the Quran.

57. Quran, Sura 2, verse 180.

The Quran is being used by Muslims to gain power, justify their exploitation, killing, and servitude to foreigners, justify their bowing down (before outsiders) and opening up (for outsiders). You are Muslims, so you exploit the Quran for personal goals. Do you think yourself more pious than the Muslim Brothers, Takfir wa Hijra, Sultan Abd al-Hamid, Abd al-Majid, Sheikh Abd al-Rahman, Abd al-Norman, or Abd al-McMillan?

Therefore, April 15, 1991 according to the western calendar was the day of the feast (Eid al-Fitr). The prayers had to be held in Mecca at 6:50 a.m. at the sanctuary and at 6:00 at the sanctuary of the Prophet. All Muslims had to observe the time differences without argument.

General Norman Schwarzkopf

Mecca, Saudi Arabia—protected by air, land, and sea.

Prayer on the Last Friday

Next Friday will be the last Friday in the month of Ramadan, no matter when the month ends. Thus, Muslims from the southern Philippines, northern Thailand, Malaysian archipelago (except Sarawak) and out to Nigeria... to one-fourth of Cameroon, three-fifths of Malawi, and one-fourth plus three-sixteenths of South Africa are required to pray in the mosque on this last Friday.

Muslims, without exception, are called to

prayer, *light and heavy armed*.[58] The full prayer will be given later on in this article. It was discovered only recently by means of cobalt rays, and helps the one who learns, teaches, or recites it to do away with all types of modern science, and especially applied sciences. How ridiculous we were when we caused schools, institutes, vocational training centres, and universities to spread throughout the country, and this also includes prefabricated and travelling schools. We insisted that each child have a chair in a classroom, so that we could conquer ignorance and literacy. We favoured absorbing modern science so that we could build progress and face the challenges of the enemy. We were ridiculous because we did not make the same effort to search for the old texts, which contained the profound secrets of orders and rites, the members of sects who disappeared over the ages, such as Ibn Taymiyya and Ibn Kathir.[59]

We were wrong when we created iron and steel industries and constructed chemical and

58. A reference to Quran, Sura 9, verse 41.
59. Medieval Muslim theologian-philosophers, sources of inspiration for many twentieth-century Islamist and fundamentalist groups.

petrochemical factories, upon which we spent billions. We should do away with the Great Man-Made River, and the second phase of the iron and steel complex, do away with the Ras Lanouf complex's second phase, which involves three hundred petrochemical factories. We should save all of these millions so that we can reprint the ancient texts.

Certainly, Muslims—and I mean Arabs, lost between the Atlantic Ocean and the Gulf—were struck with fear and terror when they became certain that the children of Israel had made great gains in modern science, with American-Arab funding, and launched a satellite that took real-time pictures every second of anything they wanted to take pictures of. The Israelis were not happy when the Jewish satellite began to send its pictures to Tel Aviv and Jerusalem, especially because the satellite, at first, began to take pictures of everything happening on a daily basis in the Arab world. They became overwhelmed with pictures of camels in Mauritania, donkeys in the Sudan, as well as pictures of kings and presidents at summit conferences.

The Israelis were truly annoyed at having

to sort out so many pictures in order to decide which of the things that were pictured were useless, and which constituted a danger to the state of Israel. They had to refocus the satellite to take pictures of selected targets only; they programmed it not to take pictures of camels, donkeys, and other such items. They then began to receive pictures of Rabta, Tajura, Tarhuna, Bou Kamash, Qasr Ahmad, the High Dam, the great man-made river, Pas Lanouf. Then, they began to see pictures of Muaytiga, a ten-year-old girl, playing in front of her house:[60] Sana;[61] Uqba Bin Nafi,[62] the tall bearded, brown-skinned one, wearing a green turban. Pictures of an Arabia, sitting in the open air, with men and women around her, veiled. Pictures of Nasser, waiting for Egypt. We know that Israel has made nuclear bombs and long-range missiles to carry them. They make warplanes, and have begun selling them to a number of countries.

This is one of the Arab nation's dangerous

60. See "Escape to Hell," footnote 19.
61. Sana Mahaydali, a Lebanese female suicide-bomber who undertook a mission against Israeli occupation forces in 1985.
62. A seventh-century Muslim military commander who oversaw the Islamicization of North Africa.

fronts of confrontation. It requires a revolutionary program to marshal all resources for the sake of working and researching so that an extremely high state of readiness may be achieved, and the consequences borne, to save a nation subject to danger and humiliation. However, the pious men of this nation have been studying Islamic law, being taught by clergy from Afghanistan, India, and Britain, such as Nabahani, Sayyid Qutbzada (an Iranian originally from India with Egyptian nationality),[63] Muhammad Asad, Hawa, Yakan (originally from Turkey), Mirza and Bahauddin (from Persia), Jacques Berque and Garaudy.[64] They have a high, unshakable opinion of these men's learning, and especially of Qutbzada, Nabahani, Black Dodge, who took the name Muhammad when he converted to Islam. They were promised that they would enter Paradise, as it was noted in a speech by Zeinab, and in their confessions in the book "Investigations and Confutations."

Anyway, what is important is that people of

63. A reference to Sayyid Qutb, Egyptian ideologist of the Muslim Brotherhood, executed in 1966.
64. French Marxist philosopher who converted to Islam.

this nation, some of whom belong to the Muslim Brotherhood Party, Islamic Liberation Party, the Repentance and Return to God movement, Jihad against Muslims, Call to and Defence of America—some of these people have gained the attention of youth, drawing them to this dangerous secret. They spent long sleepless nights engaging in scientific research. They excavated in old, yellowing tomes and found that prayer on the last Friday of Ramadan was a guarantee that all hellish plots against them would be foiled, and the consequences of modern science and new technology would be abolished. If we consider what the Party of God coalition has to say, we see that there is no need for educating our children in schools and technical institutes, or universities. Let them stay on the sidewalks, selling cigarettes out in the fresh air, peddling gum to adults. The important thing is to memorize the prayer whose text is printed below, on the condition that everyone take part—all Muslims in the areas already mentioned except for the places that have been excepted.

The prayer is as follows:

They shall not see... they shall not see.[65]

This is to be repeated one thousand times per minute on the last Friday of the month of Ramadan, followed by the word "Amen." This prayer has been tested for accuracy, and is able to make the Jews unable to see their vital targets in the Arab world, such as the Rabta medicine factory... and the Arabs themselves.

This prayer will certainly blind the Jewish satellite. A member of the Muslim Brotherhood working at the Rabta plant secretly told the Americans about the factory's real nature of work. This made the Americans move their fleets to confront Libya once again. However, with the utterance of this prayer one thousand times a minute followed by Amen, in front of the investigators, the Americas were in fact rendered unable to see the factory, let alone the Israeli satellite, which only hovers above Libya, Algeria, and Iraq. So, America did not bomb the factory, despite all those massed forces, and neither did the Israelis, up until the time of writing of this article.

65. A false reference to Quran, Sura 36, verse 91, and Sura 2, verse 17.

Another type of magical protection is reading the book "In the Shadow of the Quran,"[66] and not the Quran itself. According to the Muslim Brotherhood, the Quran is only one book, while "In the Shadow of the Quran" is actually ten books.

As it is no doubt clear to you, these books do not give the reader any spare time to read books on science or other empty pursuits such as chemistry, maths, and physics; meanwhile, there is the condition that you stay secluded in homes and mosques.

O believers, may God grant you wisdom, imagine if every Muslim from Jakarta to Marrakesh (except the areas mentioned above) remained secluded in his home, how great and mighty the prayer would be. It would be invincible, especially since it cannot be detected by the enemy's detection apparatuses; it would not appear on their screens, unlike planes, ships, and missiles.

Begin teaching your children the books of

66. By Sayyid Qutb.

the Muslim Brotherhood and the Return to God and Liberation Party. Print them and reprint them and shut yourselves up in mosques and at home studying them till Judgment Day. Their titles show you clearly how effective they are: "Religious Statutes on Growing Beards and Smoking," "Decisions of the Sunna on Using Shampoo and Henna," "Fundamentals of Entering Heaven for Free." There are also the books of Ibn Taymiyya, which explain the wisdom of eating with three fingers, eating while in a reclining position, or eating from wooden and metal plates. And do not forget the prayer mentioned above: it is especially for the military wing of the Democratic Brotherhood Islamic Party, and concerns counter-strategies. It is also related to a prayer for the economy, a simple invocation that you only need to recite a mere one hundred times second. It has been thoroughly tested, and is effective against prices rising without justification, and against exploitation that takes place without support from a revolutionary theory, or even a revolutionary party. It goes like this:

"O God, protect government workers from shop owners, and protect big merchants from little revolutionaries. If things become incomprehensible, the merchants and revolutionaries are responsible. Forgive those who cause prices to rise, and make dinars as expensive as dollars."

Meanwhile, those who want to unite the Arab nation so that it will become strong and achieve victory over the enemy, must stand behind the imam at the mosque on that special Friday and repeat: "O God, our weakness is known to you. Our fate is in your hands, and we have no genie's ring to help us. You know that the Jews and the Christians have travelled towards you in their missiles and satellites, while we refrain from joining them in their blasphemy by invading space. We implore you for help."

O believers, this is what the various, united Islamic parties call you to. The Muslim Brotherhood Party, Islamic Liberation Party, the Repentance and Return to God movement, Islamic Call and Defence Party. You cannot achieve any progress, or enter the modern age, exit your backwardness, or liberate Palestine, or at least destroy the enemy bases which target their missiles at Arab capitals. You cannot achieve any of this without going back to the ancient, yellowing texts. Go back two thousand years, so that we can remember who killed the Caliph Othman,[67] because the one responsible should be brought to justice. There is also the matter of who killed Hussein,[68] and was he or Muawiya[69] more deserving of succeeding to the caliphate of Islam? What about comparing between the qualifications of Yezid and Hussein?[70] We must ascertain exactly the number of those who attacked Othman and what time this monstrous crime took place. Go back to the books of Ibn Taymiyya and Ibn Kathir, Yakan, Hawa, Sayyid Qutbzada, Lowery, al-Mawdudi, so that we can be sure of the fundamentals required for achieving progress, solving administrative and economic problems, treating the problem of low oil prices as result of the Christians' discovery of alternative energy sources. How to implement article 51 of the United Nations Charter, which is designed to

67. The third caliph of Islam.
68. The grandson of the fourth caliph Ali, killed by forces of Yazid, son of Muawiya, and second calif of the Omayyad dynasty in a dispute over the succession to the caliphate. Part of the ethic of Shia Islam is based on drawing inspiration from the martyrdom of Hussein.
69. The first caliph of the Omayyad dynasty.
70. Muawiya and Ali's sons, between whom the succession to the caliphate was in dispute.

combat star wars, guerrilla wars, and electronic wars.

How can we move ahead, while we still do not know who should have succeeded his father as caliph—al-Hadi or al-Mahdi? Al-Amin or al-Mamoun?[71] Was the camel of Ali, may God preserve him, white or brown? Was Othman's shirt made of cotton or nylon?[72]

All of these fundamental facts are found in reactionary, I mean traditional, books. Meanwhile, your modern Islamist parties call on people to study these books thoroughly, even if you are forced to get your eyes checked and buy glasses. Perhaps some of you might ridicule my argument as blasphemy or apostasy, but which person in his right mind, living on the brink of the twenty-first century, would not be alarmed by these critical issues? How can we enter this new century while we do not even know why people prefer to eat

---

71. al-Amin and al-Mamoun, the sons of the caliph Haroun al-Rashid.
72. The bloodstained "shirt" of Othman, the third caliph, was held up by his followers at Friday prayers following his assassination. Othman's partisans attempted to incite Muslims against Ali, who they claimed was responsible for the act.

using five fingers, while using three fingers is in fact quite wise, and why you should not lick your fingers, lick the plate, or eat food that has fallen on the floor. Consult the book "Book of the Righteous" by the Imam Zakariyya, page 297, chapter 109; should a beard be dyed with henna or shampoo?! Should a Muslim woman's scarf be made by machine or by hand? If an unbeliever such as an Indian or Pole has made it, should she wear it?

May God guide Muslims to the right path, lead them to light one another, call each other unbelievers, be disunited so that they can ally with the Christians and Jews against each other. You are always present to hear our prayer! Unite the Muslims under the banners of Washington and Tel Aviv. Make them, their women, their children, and their riches a booty to be distributed among Muslims fairly and equally, with no distinction between left and right... Amen.

The Prayerless Friday

Unfortunately, all of the world's Muslims could not agree to pray together on the last Friday of the month of Ramadan. If they had, their prayer would have shaken the Zionist entity and NATO to their very foundations. It might have even brought down the Israeli satellite, but unfortunately, they could not agree to pray together. The Islamic Liberation Party set down the condition that their followers had to participate in the prayer on that day and the head of their party would become caliph of all Muslims, with prayers in his name read out at all mosques in the Islamic world: "May God aid the caliph of the Muslims, head of the Islamic Liberation Party, and bless his wives and children and enable them to succeed him." Also, if he should become unwell, prayers for his recovery would be said in all mosques in the Islamic world. Also, you should all know that what is forbidden to you is permitted to him, while your wives and children are his legal possession. There was also the condition that the members of the party's politburo—a Palestinian and two Jordanians, one of Turkish and one of Kurdish origin—should be considered descendants of the Prophet. If you mention their names, you must say: "May God be pleased with them; may God preserve the members of the Islamic Liberation Party politburo, and may He promise them entry to heaven whatever may come to pass."

The Islamic Liberation Party also set down the condition that its followers and its followers' followers and its henchmen's henchmen participate in the prayer together on the last Friday, taking the place of the Muslim Brotherhood Party. They demanded that this party be disbanded and its relationship with West German intelligence be severed, since there was a political crisis between Great Britain and non-Great West Germany about modernizing nuclear missiles. When the Islamic Liberation Party was asked about the connection between Muslims on the last Friday of Ramadan and Britain and Germany, the party spokesman said, "The nature of the struggle makes this necessary. The Islamic Liberation party cannot go against God's religion, violate its oaths, or sever its commitments. It has been historically and religiously committed to the people of the Book[73] such as British intelligence, from the days of the occupation of Palestine to Judgment Day. The party is grateful to General Glubb and Hajj Lawrence of Arabia for helping to establish it, may God bless their souls and their tombs in Bournemouth and Brevington in the south of England."

When the followers of the Muslim Brothers heard these conditions, they rose up and burnt the books of Nabahani, saying that the Islamic

73. "People of the Book" refers to Jews and Christians, whose religions are viewed by Islam as forerunners of the Prophet Muhammad's message. Below Gadaffi mentions Lawrence of Arabia, who participated in the Arab revolt during World War I against the Ottoman Empire, and John Bagot Glubb, the British general who headed Jordan's Arab Legion (national army) until 1956.

Liberation Party had been in the service of Mossad since 1936, and that its followers were Mossad agents. Every six months, financial help from Mossad would arrive via Jordan, and this party was formed of Palestinian agents of British intelligence since the days of the British mandate in Palestine. They said that this party was formed to prevent Muslims from liberating Palestine, and that the goal of the party's president was to achieve his dream of and obsession with becoming caliph of all Muslims, if only for one month, so that all mosques in the Islamic world would invoke his name during Friday prayers.

The Islamic Liberation Party responded to the Muslim Brotherhood's attacks by accusing them of being involved in the misinterpretation of the Quran in the book by Sayyid Qutbzada[74] (who was of Indian origin), "In the Shadow of the Quran." The goal of this action was to negate Abd al-Nasser's credentials to be president of Egypt, and assert those of Hassan al-Banna,[75] even though he was dead at the time, because al-Banna had learned the Quran by heart while quite young... never mind that he had forgotten it after

74. That is, Sayyid Qutb.
75. The founder of the Muslim Brotherhood in Egypt.

he became an adult. Abd al-Nasser, meanwhile, had not learned the Quran by heart. The goal of this interpretation of the Quran in "In the Shadow of the Quran" involved intervening in the conflict over power in Egypt during the 1940s and 1950s. It had no connection to the Quran, religion, God, or Libya. Religion was used for this end; the Quran was interpreted wrongly on purpose, in order to demonstrate that a certain group of Egyptians was justified in taking power.

The Islamic Liberation Party then burned the books of al-Mawdudi,[76] announcing that they were absurd. How could a foreigner teach us Arabs about our religion? We were the ones who helped him convert to Islam; we were his teachers and spiritual guides. They said, "It would be absurd for an Arab to be taught at the feet of a foreigner about the religion of Muhammad the Arab Prophet, *in the plain Arabic language.*"[77] They set down the condition that the Muslim Brotherhood Party must sever its ties to America's intelligence service, and specifically with Colonel John Palmer. They apologized for having to reveal these secrets, but explained that it was an eye for

76. A Pakistani fundamentalist thinker.
77. Reference to Quran, Sura 16, verse 103.

an eye and a tooth for a tooth and the one who began it should take the blame.

Groups such as Atonement and Flight from and to Palestine, Jihad against the People of Ejdabia, the Islamic Call to Destroy the Industrial Complex at Ras Lanouf,[78] took part in arguments about these dangerous and sensitive issues, which might lead to miracles such as desalinating sea water and using it in agriculture, converting solar power into energy, and perhaps turning stone into wool. These groups then apostatized both the Muslim Brotherhood Party and the Islamic Liberation Party, describing them as reactionaries, lackeys of imperialism, hypocrites, and libertines. The followers of these two parties were unable to meet the challenges thrown down by these new movements, such as breaking their eyeteeth, walking a distance of 25 kilometres carrying a bag of sand weighing 25 kilograms once a week, fasting 45 days instead of 30, or going six months without bathing, shaving, brushing their teeth, or clipping their fingernails, or getting married without performing the required legal formalities such as signing a wedding document (following

78. Gadaffi is sarcastically adding to the standard names of Islamist movements.

the example of Mirzada, may peace be upon him).

When the Muslim Brotherhood Party and the Islamic Liberation Party heard about these new parties appearing on the scene, they got together and supported a religious fatwa against them. They approved it officially with the big toe prints from the right foot, of the Islamic World League in Mecca, with branches in Washington (may God bless his soul), Jerusalem, and the Shemlan Institute.[79] This was done in order to put an end to the sterile argument about religion, which should not be gone into very deeply. One should exploit this argument only to gather together a band of simple followers, and use them as a cover in front of the masses. They also threatened these new groups to expose the fact that they had come to the Arab world from non-Arab countries, and were to be used against the Arab nation in the name of religion to destroy Arab nationalism, paving the way for the control over the region by Israeli or Persian nationalism. They would also be used to combat the radical social progressive trend by an unrealistic Islamic

79. The United Kingdom's language institute in Lebanon where it trained its foreign service operatives.

trend, as per the secret agreement with the Central Intelligence Agency and Mossad. The deal was to exchange the Islamic trend for the Islamic religion, and to maintain that the Atonement and Flight movement was originally from Pakistan, that the Call and Jihad movement came from Afghanistan, Iran, and India, and that these regions were the birthplace of the groups such as the Assassins, the freethinkers, and western intelligence organizations hostile to Islam and the Arab nation.

They went on to say that these movements were an extension of the Qadyaniyya, Ahmadiyya, and the Bahais,[80] whose founders pretended to be prophets, and finally gave up the religion of Muhammad, replacing it with their own sects. Instead of Islam, there would be movements such as Atonement and Flight, Call and Jihad, etc. So, we had to do without the participation of these parties and their followers and henchmen on the prayer of the last Friday of Ramadan as a result of differences among them which cannot be resolved until Doomsday.

80. The United Kingdom's language institute in Lebanon where it trained its foreign service operatives.

Unfortunately, this was not the entire extent of the problem. The Muslims of Pakistan then said, "We refuse to participate because for Pakistan, as an Islamic state, occupied territory means Kashmir and our deadly enemy is India, and not "Israel." The Muslims of India, meanwhile, did not agree to participate either, because they did not agree with us about who the enemy is, or what the purpose of the jihad is. The real enemy of the Muslims of Indonesia is Malaysia, a hostile Muslim state on the borders of Muslim Indonesia, although the traditional enemy is Japan. For the Muslims of the Philippines, occupied territory is not Palestine, but Mindanao. It is Manila, and not Tel Aviv, that has negative connotations for them. Even worse, there are Israeli embassies and interests sections representing the Zionist enemy in these Muslim countries.

It thus becomes clear that Israel is the enemy of only the Arab nation, and that America is allied with Muslim countries, thus serving the interests of Israel; but this is something which we fail to recognize. Islam does not constitute a single political, economic, or military unit. We find Turkey, a Muslim nation, which ruled the

Islamic world for 600 years in the name of religion, a member in NATO, which is led by America. Turkey's relations with Israel are very good. Muslim African nations have no problem with asking western Christian nations for help against us, and happily allow their military bases to sit atop their Islamic soil. Suffice it to say that the Comoros Islands have given up one of their islands to France as a gesture of thanks after it helped return Hajj Ahmad Abdullah to power. The Muslim inhabitants of Mayotte have voted, meanwhile, to join Christian France.

All of these painful realities remind us that the Muslims of the world cannot fight with us against a common enemy, because the enemy of the Arabs is the friend of the non-Arab Muslims, and vice versa. So, there is no hope for political or military unity from now until Judgment Day. There are no common economic interests between us at all. Turkey is tied to Israel due to tourism and trade, while in terms of its labour force it is tied to West Germany, a member of the European Common Market, despite Islam. The Muslims of Malawi and Liberia, it turns out, are very pro-American. The only ones who sympathize with us have been revolutionaries from throughout the world, but they are non-Muslim. They said, "We see that the Arabs have been wronged and humiliated by Zionism and imperialism, and that Palestine is Arab, and has been occupied since 1948." But we, for our part, rejected their participation because they are not Muslims. At the same time, we have realized that Muslims are not Arabs, and that Arabs are Muslims.

Therefore, the last Friday of Ramadan passed without prayer being held, because we found that each nation had its own religion, and its own prophet. Each one has its own future, and destiny, as well as its own enemy, and interests. Anything other than this is pure deceit and foolishness. The Arab nation would have to taste the bitter cup of humiliation alone, the extermination of its people by its enemy, while its enemy was the ally and friend of non-Arab Muslim nations. Settling these differences would be a flight of fancy.

As for the followers of the Islamic Liberation Party and the Muslim Brotherhood Party, as well as Atonement and Flight, the Islamic Call and Jihad against Innocent Believers,

we let them poke around, like chickens, among
the books of Ibn Taymiyya, and the latest
illustrious fatwa printed by the CIA. They said,
"We will participate in jihad against the enemy as
soon as we have finished reading Imam al-
Ghazali,[81] and figure out whether death is a
winged creature or goes on all fours. And if it is
the latter, is it bigger than a donkey and smaller
than a horse? And if the grapes which fell upon
Khobeib Ibn Uday, when he was a prisoner of the
unbelievers in Mecca, came from Venus or
Mercury?" Because there were no grapes in
Mecca, although Ibn Taymiyya, the venerable
sheikh of Islam, confirms that grapes would fall
daily on Khobeib. Um Ayman, meanwhile, who
was about to die of thirst between Mecca and
Medina, and was fasting, was visited by a bowl of
parsley soup, and a bucket of mineral water
labelled Evian. She drank the water, and never
felt thirst again as long as she lived. Taymiyya
goes on to say that Khalid Bin al-Walid,[82] while
besieging a well-fortified Byzantine fort, asked
them to surrender, and they replied, "We will
surrender if you drink a glass of poison." He
drank two glasses of cyanide, and was not

81. Twelfth-century theologian.
82. Muslim general during the first wars of conquest.

bothered in the least by a single bit of his insides. This is what Ibn Taymiyya, the sheikh of Islam, wrote in his famous book, which is considered the constitution of the Atonement and Flight movement, the Islamic Call and Jihad, the Brotherhood, and the Islamic Liberation Party.

We are now waiting for the leaders of these parties to determine the exact nature of death; is it a winged or legged creature? How did the grapes fall upon the prisoners in Mecca, which supposedly had no grapes? How did the soup and Evian water come to Um Ayman? These scientific studies will lead to changes in the world and its culture and philosophical presuppositions, which are built on empty concepts such as gravity, drift, trigonometry, solid geometry, centrifugal force, and logarithms.

We await the results of this scientific research by the Islamist parties, which are actually imported,[83] and related to Magianism and hidden-inner[84] philosophies; we should help

83. "Imported" in the sense of non-authentic, or borrowed from foreign ideologies and systems of power.
84. In Arabic, *batiniyya* refers to hidden or inner meaning of religious texts.

them in reprinting the books of Ibn Taymiyya, Ibn Kathir, and al-Mawdudi, with dazzling titles such as "Religion and Conjugal Relations between Spouses," "Religious Statutes Concerning Smoking and Growing Beards," "More Views on the Prophet and Polygamy," "Hymns Sung during Intercourse in the Afterlife," "Khalid Ibn al-Walid's Method of Eating Dried Meat." This latter book is important, since we must learn how he ate dried meat, and not about how he gained victory over the Byzantines or about his martial strategy. There is also the book "The Wisdom of Eating with Three Fingers," by Ibn Taymiyya.

Do not be sullen, O believers, because on the last Friday of Ramadan in the following year, or the one after that, or after that, we might arrive at the knowledge of these amazing scientific realities.

The Musahharati during the Day

All of us know and like the musahharati.[85] Even the little children, who like Ramadan, would look forward to hearing him wake people up with his simple drum and its beautiful rhythms, accompanying the voice we have become accustomed to hearing every year... every night during the nights of the month of Ramadan. We would all hear those lovely calls

85. During Ramadan, the musahharati walks around a neighbourhood or group of neighbourhoods, beating a drum and calling upon people to rise and take the *suhur*, or pre-dawn meal.

and pleasant words, while children would repeat them long afterward. We would use those expressions on certain occasions, when they seemed applicable, saying "Wake up, sleeper" whenever we wanted to implore someone to get up and be active. May God reward the musahharati for his humble efforts and repeated calls at the end of the night, waking us so that we may have our pre-dawn meal, preparing us for what might be a long day of fasting.

The musahharati is a rare character, and there are certainly not many like him. He is a true "one of a kind," and has abilities that most people do not possess. His responsibilities are of the moral variety, involving the conscience, kindness, and self-discipline. His purpose is to wake up those who slumber; his pains are great and he walks great distances, moving about alleys and lanes to wake up the inhabitants. He might trip and stumble many times, but he will never fall down on the job. His mood is not affected as a result; he continues on his path, fingering his prayer beads and calling out the ninety-nine names of God, and letting everyone hear his wake-up call.

What is also amazing is that the musahharati needs no one to wake him. He is the one who wakes people up, and unlike them, needs no drum or repeated calls to be awakened. The musahharati as a character inspires wonder in all of us. Truly, who wakes him so that he may wake us? Doesn't he sleep? Of course he does. The musahharati is a human being like us, and he is affected by weariness. He sleeps, like us, and gets sick, like us, or at least needs sleep and rest, like us. The amazing thing is that his waking-time is when it is time for all to sleep. He carries out his holy mission while others are sound asleep, in a state of inactivity and rest. He walks in the darkness, in the deep of the night, stumbling and continuing on, falling and getting up. Perhaps it is for this reason that some of us do not like the musahharati, in the way we do not like the muezzin who performs the call to prayer at dawn.

The call to prayer, however, is repeated so often that we become used to it. It is not a rare occurrence, but takes place from morning until evening. The muezzin announces the prayer from where he is; he might call to prayer while he is reclining in bed, via a loudspeaker. He does not irritate people, because he does not move around and pass in front of their doors, as the musahharati does. The prayer, moreover, is made up of certain memorized phrases with nothing new or added to them. But the musahharati moves about and is creative, beating his drum and calling out, invoking the name of God. He can say what he deems fit to wake up those who are asleep. He can repeat his call and prayers, but in a pleasing way, a way that children like; so much so that they even try to memorize these phrases and repeat them later, even though they may not understand the meaning.

The musahharati's voice is magical, and like magic, does not need annoying loudspeakers, which can be frightfully deafening, like the ones used by the muezzins in Malta.

In any case, we may both love and hate the musahharati. Even the ones who hate him for depriving them of their final hours of sleep, and getting them ready for the next day, speak well of him on the day of fasting, though they have already spoken ill of him.

This concerns the musahharati at night— but what about the musahharati during the day?

Part II

Essays

Long Live the State for the Wretched!

Death to the Incapable... Until Revolution

Is Communism Truly Dead?

Once Again, An Urgent Call to Form a Party

Long Live the State
for the Wretched!

How sweet will be the victory of the wretched, and how great! How beautiful their dawn, when it comes forth and shines without requesting permission—how magnificent will the sun be on the day of the wretched ones, when it dazzles the world, rising into the sky without ceasing. You will be happy, wretched ones, on the day of your victory under the radiant sun, and will hear the music of the birds on the dawn of that great day.

How sweet will the songs be on that golden

day, and how brilliant the golden sun of the wretched as it blazes. How sweet this dangerous dream—that hopes will be realized, that wishes become true. That a dream will become reality, that the wretched of the earth will have their state. Freedom will sing to them her eternal song, and the strings will sound without their instruments, and anthems will sing out by themselves! The beasts of burden will fly on wings of joy, hovering upon the pleasant wind— how beautiful will that day be: the day of resurrection for the wretched!

The trumpet will sound, announcing the dawn of the renaissance;[86] the living will embrace one another and laugh, laugh until the tears come. The laughter of joy, tears streaming from their eyes, wounded and swollen from torture. Few are the tears that they have shed, few because they are forbidden from expressing their pains, even through tears. They had to absorb disgrace after disgrace, drink down bitterness after bitterness, without even having the right to cry. The warm and bitter tears accumulated until they cooled, hardened, and

86. Reference to Quran, Sura 20, verse 102.

finally froze, leaving eyes cracked and swollen.

But on that memorable renaissance-day for the masses or the wretched, the day their dream of a state was proclaimed, on that day their frozen eyes warmed. In their very eyes, where the movement of blood and life had been forbidden, movement returned, quickened, and gave out heat until the sores[87] and swelling vanished. On that day, from these exiled eyes, tears of joy are flowing out like the winter rain. Wash your tired and exhausted faces, in the rich water of tears, the divine tears of holiness. How pure this water, and how holy a liquid it is, warm and soothing. Now that their long-sought-after state is here, let the wretched now run and play, and jump. Let them pick flowers, swim in the pure air, and fly on wings of joy. Let them bathe in their very sweat, pouring out of their bodies from the excess of joy, and long-missed activity. Let them discover the grace of their bodies, by merely looking, and seeing how beautiful their bodies are.

Graceful bodies, coloured by torture, and valuable torn and patched-up clothes. Who owns

87. See Quran, Sura 69, verse 36.

such rags but you, the wretched? Who wears them without noticing them but you? The smell of these torn garments is pure, and the odour of their bodies refreshing, a smell emanating from unquenched bodies. Bodies without insides, the angel-like bodies of those who drink the pure water of valleys and streams. Bodies nourished by air in the outdoors, free of any air conditioning or other artificial devices. Bodies that do not eat anything forbidden, nor drink anything impure or unclean.[88] Let the air be filled with these pure odours; they are a balsam for the wounds of the ozone layer, torn by the fumes of the mighty and powerful, by the luxury items of the rich and wealthy.

Sing, wretched ones, if your state has been attained, and raise your suppressed voices. Clear your raspy-voiced throats, and let your silent tongues speak, open up your long-closed minds. Sing out anthems of victory, and raise your fluttering flags high in the sky. Do not forget to mend them first, for they are torn, and do not forget to colour them, for they are colourless now. You are free, so choose the colour that you wish,

88. Literally, "filth"; Quran, Sura 69, verse 36.

or use a mixture of many different colours—write the slogans of your choosing. The sky will be beautiful when the flags of the wretched fly high, and the horizon will stretch out limitlessly before their newborn state.

The world will become quite an attentive listener when the echoes of that great festival reach it. The entire world will crane its neck as it seeks out the source of that musical sound. All of the birds will share in your joy—even the owl and the raven[89] will delight in the victory of the wretched ones. All of the earth's poor creatures and all of its refugees will rejoice, happy in their victory. Nature itself will participate, laughing and happily embracing your rejoicing on that day, clasping your very dancing and crying out.

A splendid, divine procession, and a wondrous halo around the litter at the wedding you celebrate, wretched ones. The wedding litter sways upon the back of the camel, the sign of eternal destiny, and lights up the far horizon, scattering the darkness before it.

89. Birds portenting bad luck or evil in Arab culture.

The clouds will scatter before this splendour, and the bright sun will appear after your long night has fled. The air will become pure, and the sun will contentedly allow all of the distant stars to approach, unafraid, and twinkle like pearls.[90] The stars will come nearer the lowest heaven,[91] so that the sun becomes more dazzling. More lights for the wedding celebration, and new colours of the spectrum. For the first time there will be more than one spectrum, increasing the colours seven-fold. Let everything rejoice, let everyone empty their gun-barrels in celebration—why not, for it is the victory-day of the wretched ones? They have their state now, their sun and their earth. *The angels rank in rank,*[92] giving their blessing to this glorious day, as both the visible and invisible worlds[93] do the same. The sea is silent in a salute to the wretched, then the waves crash together in applause. The wind ceases, to let the victory procession pass. The storms break in a dance for

90. See Quran, Sura 55, verse 58.
91. See Quran, Sura 67, verse 5.
92. See Quran, Sura 89, verse 22.
93. According to Kazimirski and Masson, "al-thaqlan" (here translated as "the visible and invisible worlds") could mean humans and djinns; for Lane, it could mean Arabs and non-Arabs.

the wretched. The thunder stops, to glorify God, who has granted victory to the wretched. The lightning unsheathes its sword and salutes them. Millions of suns draw nigh[94] to light with their cold fire millions and millions of candles—candles celebrating the victory of the wretched. The entire earth turns into a moon, lit by millions of candles in their blessed oil lamps, which do not become extinguished.[95]

I do not want you to become men of power, wretched ones, for this will only make you worse off, and leave you with the stigma of being a collaborator. I do not want you to become wealthy, for this will cause you harm as well; it will brand you with the sign of the rich, for which there is no cure. I do not want you to become sheikhs or learned men of religion, for it will leave you marked by the sign of the charlatan, of the ignorant. You will not be arrogant; let others act in this way. You will not be haughty; let the devils act in such fashion. The state of the wretched is alone in having no borders, for borders mean limits, and the wretched do not have such restrictions. Borders

94. Quran, Sura 55, verse 31.
95. Reference to Quran, Sura 24, verse 35.

involve problems, smuggling, and it is not right for the wretched to involve themselves in trouble-making. Over borders there are wars and flights. The wretched should not engage in warfare or be forced to flee. They have no weapons or arms, for arms and weapons are for killers, soldiers, and aggressors. The wretched do not attack, for they are peaceful people. They do not need police or guards, or warning devices and bells. Such things, such devices for hegemony, are for those who have doubt in their hearts. The wretched have their wonderful latent characteristics, although they remain captive. Their desires are sublime heavenly—if they were allowed to spread they would make the very universe fragrant—and can cure any disease.

There is no aggression in the state of the wretched; their pure bodies have no such connection to this evil. With no envy, ambition, or greed, there is no need for police and soldiers. The wretched provide their own security and contentment. You are pure, and uncorrupted by the world of iniquity. You are the pure creatures of creation, and you will survive, for yours is glory. Survival of the best, of the most beautiful, of the most beneficial. You are more righteous than any other righteous and more beautiful than beauty because you are millions upon millions, and beauty is but one, and alone.

Your lives involve a greater good, and you are not self-interested; do not pay attention *to their doubt,*[96] for *their stratagem will come to naught.*[97] Do not pay them heed: with dignity, and a smile on your faces, let pass their *senselessness.*[98] If you inherit the earth,[99] wretched ones, it will not be as it is now, the land of *those who are effete with luxury*[100] and oppressors, hypocrites, and prevaricators, the land of corruption, a corrupt land fit only for the corrupt. This is the true secret for their hating you: you are not of this world, you are not wealthy, and for this they hate you. You are not oppressors, and for this they hate you. You are not pretenders, so they hate you. You are not hypocrites or liars, and for this they hate you.

96. Quran, Sura 6, verse 2; Sura 44, verse 50; Sura 19, verse 34. Pickthall's translation renders it "their disputing"; in Sura 2, verse 147; Sura 3, verse 60; Sura 19, verse 94, etc. it is rendered as "wavering."
97. Quran, Sura 105, verse 2.
98. Quran, Sura 25, verse 72.
99. See Quran, Sura 21, verse 105.
100. Quran, Sura 56, verse 105.

Only a corrupt state is created in a corrupt land.

Those such as you have no status in such a world, no common language with its inhabitants. Like you they see what others do not, walk toward what they do not, say what others do not, eat and drink what others do not, wear what others do not, sleep where others do not, and dream of what others do not. For this they have called you the wretched, because you are poor, simple folk. Because you cannot dance for money, or act, or be hypocritical. Because they forced you, in order for you to stay alive, to dance with no shame, to sing like a parrot, to act the parts of devils in the costume of the pious. Who is the oppressor, then, if not the one who treats people like you wretchedly? The one who despises looks at you with hatred, and talks about you with hatred. They treat you wretchedly—and the ones who are the most wretched in their souls have imparted this description to you!

Wretchedness is a stone with which they hit you. An arrow launched at you, a burden[101] they have cast upon you. A robe they have dressed you

---

101. Reference to Quran, Sura 53, verse 38.

with. The one who bears this stone, this arrow, this burden, this robe, is weighed down by wretchedness. As for you, is it your fault if the guilty ones have cast their wretchedness, cast its stones and arrows upon you? Is it your fault if the ones who are burdened with it or dress in it burden you with it or dress you in it? You are passive in this equation; you are completely, totally, absolutely innocent, it is not your fault that you have been made to be the passive one, while they act actively. In fact, you are the prey of these active verbs—cast, dress, give, burden. You are passively constituting the object, and they are actively constituting the subject.[102]

The true wretched ones are those who employ the stones and arrows, the robes and burdens of wretchedness. You will never be like them, and you will never treat others wretchedly at all, be assured, for your bitter and painful yet rich experience has taught you many lessons. Your travails will not befall anyone.

---

102. In the Arabic, there is a slightly longer passage involving word-play based on grammatical terms.

Do not let your conscience be troubled. You will not coerce anyone, because you are the victim of coercion by others. You will not take pleasure in making others wretched, having tasted the bitterness that has been practiced against you. You know better than others that the meanings of words are external rather than internal, it arrives rather than leaves, and is objective rather than subjective. O wretched ones, you are teachers, you have the power to explain, you are authorities in the matter. You are the wise men, with your great historical experience, and you know that the ones who have inscribed wretchedness upon you have said that water is blue, a sign of true ignorance that is truly laughable. They have said that it is either fresh or salty. But you know that water itself has neither taste nor colour. Water is innocent of these attributes and characteristics, just as you are innocent of the description by others of you that you are wretched.

Therefore, let it be a great and glorious day when your state is proclaimed, for it will be the day that justice is done. The falsehoods will be proclaimed false[103] on that day, when the truths

103. Reference to Quran, Sura 8, verse 8; Sura 17, verse 81; or alternatively rendered "truth versus vanity."

are removed from their coverings. The day that all inner essences of things will become revealed. Unclothed bodies will appear and reveal their natural equality, without interference by and accommodation of anyone or anything. The day that all false justifications will be dropped, which they used as pretexts to claim that it was in fact you who were wretched. The day you will not need to passively accept reality, or comply with it because material reality exercises a control over your lives. This is what forced you to accept the position of being wretched, and toil and labour to accommodate the requirements of wretchedness. When you were obliged to accept the lies, and when you were criticized without being discomforted and felt content about the ones who treated you wretchedly, when you were easily submissive, to the point where you were quickly brought to the depths of despair—because you felt your divine essence,[104] which cannot be affected from without you felt that they were driving you toward this. Thus, in very intelligent fashion, you encouraged your tormentors to think that you liked being lowly, so they were quick to push you unresisting in that direction.

104. See Quran, Sura 30, verse 30; elsewhere rendered as "nature."

In fact, you were looking for a quick solution for your terrible state. You saw that surrendering to your tormentors without the slightest hesitation was, in the final analysis, a solution. You exaggerate the link between your destiny and theirs since you are one of the perfect complements to their lives. A kind of decorative ornament, yet one of the base things that result from their actions. One of the sins that result from their behaviour. One of the synonyms for their encumbrances. You accepted their wretched treatment, because resisting it would not have made things easy in your life with them.

Death to the Incapable... Until Revolution [105]

Poor incapable ones, how far you are from the bitter truth! You are truly envied, for you take the easiest of paths in life, and take on no hardships. You require no explanation or interpretation of anything that you care about. Everything is clear for you; there is no vagueness. You take on no responsibility for thinking about your lives, nor do you make any change in your customary and limited ways of behaviour. You

---

105. The more common type of revolutionary slogan in Arabic would be "Revolution until Death."

easily decline anything involving difficulty, sparing your bodies and your consciences any effort. You fool yourselves extremely easily, and make light of any criticism of what you do or believe. Your opinions are fixed, and changes are never made to them. You deal negatively with any unaccustomed-to position. You never accept discussion about anything you believe; you are envied for this by those who have become weary from their envy, knowing the truth of what you do.

The truly strange thing in your lives is that you not only fail, but fail to learn your lesson. Any effect on you is not taken advantage of as a useful experience, no matter how much you fail you never change. No matter how much your beliefs betray you, this is never accepted by you. You are distinguished by your inability to recognize the truth, no matter how irrefutable. What is certain is that you will reject those results that do not agree with your fixed tendencies. You rely on an order of things and ideas that are not, of course, justifiable. You make accommodations with all truths and lies as well, according to the prior beliefs that you espouse. For example, you hold the belief that magic, or a group of evil spirits, can steal the moon, and could even do so with the sun; the boldness of these hidden beings is quite dangerous! If experiments are performed in front of you that show that it is the earth's shadow which sometimes falls upon the moon and obscures it, or that the moon's shadow falls upon the sun and causes an eclipse, you do not believe it. Why? Because this is not something that you do not desire.

In fact, nothing at all will change for you. Your lives are monotonous and calm; you are submissive until the end. You take the easiest of roads, even if it means total destruction. Impotence of action covers your world, which is dreary and boringly lived. However, despite your incapability, you are capable of accommodating your world with what changes can be made in accordance with your impotence. The hard lessons of the past are forgotten. You take the surface road, the one that requires no effort. You adopt the superstitions of the past, and reject others that do not conform to the pace of your easy, trusting lives, even if there are truths at stake. You never look for the truth; this is not your concern. Rather, you resort to what suits your state of inability to act, and no more.

The sellers of nothingness have encouraged you, plundering markets and setting up cemeteries where they sell you canned air. When you open such cans, the air flies out and mixes with the atmosphere—they explain this by saying that this item is both sold and bought. The sellers of cooked earth also encouraged you, as well as the drawers on the sand, the astrologers, writers of magic spells, and exorcists. You seek help from the dead, while the living among you are unable to help. You who achieved your dreams while asleep, your *confused dreams,*[106] while you are unable to achieve anything while awake. When you fail in your lives, you postpone success until the after-life. If you by chance are defeated through your own action, you explain this by saying that it was not really due to this action, so that you will not burden yourselves with the duty of resisting it. If you fail to defend yourself, you explain this by saying that it is outside your volition, the reason for it is an outside actor, so that the responsibility will fall upon another. If you fail due to a reason that you would not like to be external, or self-caused, then you say that it is luck.

106. See Quran, Sura 12, verse 44, and Sura 21, verse 5.

Although the world of the incapable has no meaning and no effectiveness, is null and void and silly, and although they have no positive effect in life... and although they are of no consequence, and are parasitic and trusting in their everyday lives, irresponsible and not serious, in their frail, comic world... in their empty, superficial world although they justify things, are apologists, and insignificant, and although they create nothing and change nothing... despite all of this, the world of these incapable ones is the richest, most fertile, most teeming, and full of literary meaning. For the world of these people has its culture; it has an ability to accumulate psychologies and narratives of literature, myth, and metaphysics. If it were not for this, the world would be completely material and utterly dry and calculating. It would be multiplyingly multiplied, addedly added, and divisingly divided; in structural terms it would be bottomed out and topped,[107] and made convex and concave. Without the world of these impotent actors, the world would be at its wit's end, connected and electrified and joltingly tense. Were it not for them, the human race would be active solely in a

107. These expressions are alliteratively stronger in Arabic, where they are used for effect, and not literal sense.

material sense, imprisoned between fixedness and mechanical movement, as if its hell were an inescapable prospect. The world's dictionary would be full of lifeless terms and words... atomic and modulating, chronological and inclusive, gravitating, equilibrilizing, and non-existence.

But what is truly, truly beautiful for those incapable and impotent ones whose lives are drowned in a sea of myth, who draw invisible pictures when they so desire, who interpret the world of force, material things, and progress in the way that suits them. They are heedless, unembarrassed by the frightening, empirical world. They have filled the world with their amazing dictionary, filled with gelatinous definitions and opening up limitless horizons. They have taken their imaginations farther than others; they have used their dictionary to name the world; they have explored the unending cosmos[108] where logical and involuntary miracles exist. They then make retreating actions to the unknown, unrecorded, and un-understood past; they revive this past in an attractive way; using it to interpret concrete

108. Or "without cosmic boundaries," if we consider the expression borrowed from Quran, Sura 53, verse 14.

existence in a mythical way. They find feeble meanings for it in material givens of this existence. From this sensitive point, the impotent ones succeed in exploding the meaningless dialectical revolution. The theory of superstition is in force; logic flees from the equation. Knowledge becomes foolish and insignificant. Below a brilliant, rainbow-like ornamental halo, everything finds its explanation in impotent metaphor. But these metaphors are not serious, and thus not thought out in scientific fashion. Thus, this is how the spirit of the incapable takes over the hearts of the masses, who then fall away from positions of struggle and seriousness, toward positions of easy surrender using the logic of these very incapable ones, who do not recognize the law of the self, who do not believe in themselves.

Here, the defeats find their justification in the culture of the impotence, while setbacks are explained away as bad luck. Failing to perform is justified as a lack of will. The reasons for decline are said to involve necessity; the thing or person responsible disappears, and it is understood without being believed (as in Quranic interpretation), and the pre- or post-reasoning becomes a storehouse of inexhaustible excuses used to avoid accountability.

The world of the impotent sits squatting on the straw of the life of illusion. Its law is one of renunciation and defeat, submission to all forms of plunder and pillage. It is based on deliverance from the burdens of the ready-made and moral searches, to comprehend the humiliation and justify it. It is based on a readiness to undertake hereditary or future costuming in order to flee from the conflict of the present. The incapable are always biased toward the source of the incapability. They are forgiving of being struck and slapped, and they create sick and satisfying explanations for this. They blame opportunities and circumstances, luck and hidden things, their ancestors... Mean while, their newspapers are daily filled with crossword puzzles, horoscopes, and lottery drawings. The sensing of superstitions becomes quite a sensitive practice, and attempts to justify this and reveal mysteries become deep-rooted. Anxiety is overcome, and a false sense of balance is created by checking omens, and by believing them. Dreams are interpreted, totems, pagan gods, and ancestors are entreated for help.

It is compensated for when those impotent ones oppress those more unfortunate than them, including women and children; this is a way of oppressing a projection of themselves in a search for lost balance. Entertainment then takes on the meaning of wasting time and being absorbed; culture becomes superficial, telling and exchanging jokes takes the place of good literary work and criticism. Entertainment becomes the issue that takes the place of the truth; entertainment and absurdity link up, along with unnecessary needs, sterile dependence, and social conflict and strife. Moral decadence and decay result as well. They are all the sicknesses of these incapable people, and find their explanation in the state of impotence that is lived by these people.

Revolution: when feelings of impotence penetrate every part of the life of the incapable, and they lose the feeling of impotence and the decline that it involves. When neglect, ignominy, and baseness fail to provoke, the life of the impotent reaches zero, a static level of silliness and marginality. The countdown to approaching nothingness begins, and one begins to feel the accumulated weight of this condition. The incapable are no longer able to carry out a revolution against themselves, except by having the chance to compare their lot with their opposites, by being incited[109] by someone, or by seeing the situation for themselves. The opportunity must be a good one if incitement involves visual accompaniment. It will be an especially good opportunity if the source of the impotence is befallen by an imbalance which encourages risk-taking. If the disequilibrium continues, is used properly, and is expanded by propaganda or further incitement, then the dead morale of the incapable will become filled with life.

Here, the revolution will first proceed into the self. The impotent person will begin to treat himself violently. He begins to humiliate and insult the self, until it becomes a ready-made sacrifice. He begins to present selves that the impotent have cheapened to the altar of impotence. This is the explanation for suicides, which become more frequent in the world of the impotent, for the most trivial of reasons. These people enter a phase of wandering in the desert, with series of lone, aimless, unconnected actions.

109. In the sense of being politically instigated ; "incitement" would be the task of the revolutionary committees in Libya.

Usually, this self-destructive state is accompanied by sadistic initiatives against the other, and the sacrifice is of a cow, suicide for a word, murder committed over a mere tree, divorce over the sake of a meal. The false need to place borders among the impotent, from where they live to what they eat and drink, to the area of playpens, traffic and turning, the volume level, and the sound of footsteps. Regarding the source of the impotence, each impotent person imitates other impotent people. He practices all types of superficiality and hostility against them, trying to deceive himself, convince himself that he is not like them. This is the law of life of these incapable people on any level, whether individuals, groups, or countries. The life of the impotent will continue in this manner, as long as the circumstances remain the same.

But if it is the case that the impotent have a factor in their favour, which will help them achieve salvation, then their situation can be moved from the vicious circle toward movement in a path that is not circular. The shamefaced style of the incapable could be transformed into a violent revolution against the source of impotence, and it will be violent because this source lives also in a state of chronic hatred and is moodily justified against the impotent. It does not exist in a psychological situation that allows him to comprehend the reaction, but makes it provocative and surprising. Therefore, neither party can be held responsible for the confrontation. Thus the revolution breaks out— and let death come to the impotent until revolution.

Is Communism Truly Dead?

The red flag, which was so easily taken down by one soldier from the Kremlin guard—that flag, for whom thousands of martyrs fell, downed by bullets, downed in cold battles with torture, mistreatment, and starvation in the darkness of prisons and solitary confinement in all parts of the world—the flag was dyed red with the blood of tens of millions of Russians. Under it struggled millions of people from nations that declared themselves communist, so that it would be raised over the entire earth. How did this happen, and is this the end of a

series of miraculous events or the beginning?
Will we see other historical earthquakes that
bring down all truths and assumptions? For
example, will we see Christianity fall after
people come to their senses and realize that
they were deceived when it was said to them
that Christ crucified himself to forgive the sins
of his followers, no matter what they had done.
On the basis of this, Christian countries have
killed millions of the peoples of the world, since
they had received Christ's forgiveness
beforehand.

Some people in the Christian world might
become aware of the fact that Christ's crucifying
himself for their sakes is a historical falsehood.
People will become shaken from their
Christianity, and in fact march toward the
churches in order to demolish them, breaking
crosses, scraping away the layers of ministers and
monks. They will declare that Jesus was nothing
more than a prophet of Israel, sent to inform
Israel to correct the law of Moses, no more, and
no less. Since the Jews rejected any encroachment
upon their law, which they had vowed to uphold,
they were hostile to Jesus. They cast him out and
crucified him, although in fact *they had only his*

likeness.[110] Or God took him unto Him, and raised him up to Him.

Will we see America mediate between the Libyans, with their spiritual relations and moral influence and their Iranian brothers, because the Iranians engage in mediation with their brothers the Germans? After all, they are from the same race, i.e. the Aryan race. So that the Germans, who look upon the poor Americans with sympathy, will forgive them their famous historical sin that they committed against the Germans in World War II? So that America, if the Germans accept its plea for mercy, will be ready to apologize for the landing at Normandy, and Eisenhower's landing in North Africa, so that the Germans will be able to consider that these events did not happen at all? That America was guilty, was wrong, for that historical mistake made by Roosevelt. America might send a delegation of blacks, or American Indians, since it knows how much the Libyans sympathize with them, during the days of the old imperialist delusion about Libya. To let America play upon

---

110. The Quranic explanation of the death of Jesus in Sura 4, verse 157, and also Sura 3, verse 55.

and play with the emotions of the Libyans, and help it, it said to the delegation: America would like to request the greatest number possible of Green Books, Qurans, and if possible, in English.

We see how the Fourth Reich imposes its conditions on America and Britain—the first condition is destroying their weapons under German supervision. Another is exorbitantly high compensation payments, putting it on the verge of bankruptcy—setting up a German committee in America and another one in Britain in order to permanently supervise the carrying out of these actions.

We see France enjoying illusory independence under the Fourth Reich; the French nuclear code is carried in a briefcase to Berlin. Germany rejects mediation, and imposes tyrannical tribute upon America and Britain in compensation for what they did to the German people. National socialism becomes the dominant doctrine from Poland to France.

We see the Israelis announcing their acceptance of a friendly solution that satisfies the Arabs. The first solution they accept is their distribution throughout the Arab world as protected minorities, putting their expertise at the service of the Arabs, because this will be one million times better than their staying in Palestine, as a Jewish state within sight of the frightening Fourth Reich. Without America, they will ask Libya to carry out its nation-oriented duty and assist in the implementation of this solution, because if Libya accepts it, no one will try to go it one better.

This will most certainly take place, because the signs are there, and the results are inevitable. American scientists themselves have confirmed that America will experience desertification on the one hand, and global freezing on the other. They confirmed that the fall of the Soviet Union is the reason for the change in these natural phenomena, and nature has begun to have its effects in America as well. The ethnic groups that make up America will begin to fight among themselves, like they have done in Lebanon. It was also proven that the conflict of nationalities (a social factor) was another reason for the fall of the Soviet Union. Capital will flee the fourth world, and will certainly leave America. However, we must return to the key to these mysteries—

how did the world become entangled in Marxism-Leninism?

Marx summarized human history as follows: primitive communism was the beginning, and this is correct. Man then became divided into groups, and more groups. Each group created social partnerships, with cooperative ownership of land and everything else, including marriage, which made various human races, and this is also historically correct. Then, individual ownership became established, and the superior ones constituted forms of private property, making slaves of the weak, backward, and unlucky. A slave society was then created, which was then transformed by their labours into a feudalist society. Cities were then formed, with the bourgeoisie taking the place of the feudalists. Cities then developed into capitalism, and society became divided into workers and bosses. Marx said that it was necessary to incite the workers to revolution so that they could obtain property.

Revolution took place in Czarist Russia, and was called the Soviet Union. Stalin said that in order to protect the revolution, apparatuses of oppression were necessary; they were called intelligence, external security, national security, secret police, secret service, security of the revolution, revolutionary courts, etc. Exceptional courts, military courts, political prison... all of this in terms of the security issue. On the economic side, he talked of appropriation, nationalization, sequestration, then public ownership and state ownership. And collective ownership. Finally, cooperative ownership. Then Stalin abolished the doctrine of the law of supply and demand. He abolished competition, and fixed pricing and subsidized goods appeared. The communist party was institutionalized to lead the socialist state toward communism. A group of giants, from the founder Lenin to the iron Stalin to Khrushchev and Brezhnev, assumed leadership of the party in the Soviet Union. Finally, Gorbachev, who presented the red flag to a soldier for it to be folded, perhaps... perhaps for forever.

This did not take place in the Soviet Union alone, but spread throughout practically the entire world; even in America and Britain are there communist parties. Communist countries were established in the western hemisphere as well.

It became the fashion to have revolutions or coups, even if against socialist regimes. But these actions would be marked by an iron-willed party, secret police, political prisons, exceptional courts, appropriating freedoms, apparatuses of external and internal security, national security... patriotism, nationalism, even America was affected by this. Its Central Intelligence Agency was developed, and deployed outside the country's borders. It committed acts more atrocious than those of the Soviet external security committee, which later became the KGB. Competition reached its summit between the CIA and KGB... coups, assassinations, counterfeiting money, forging identity documents and passports, buying agents, from the most worthless person to the president of a country. In order to spite Germany, a Jewish state was established in Palestine, despite the dangerous future it held for the Jews themselves, and its effects on world peace.

After the fall of the Kremlin and the end of the cold war, will all of the related effects also collapse? Will it involve the Jewish state, the party, the political prison, apparatus of suppression, appropriation of property, nationalization, sequestration, CIA, mind-set of national security and external security, etc.?

There is no doubt that the old world will fall, from America to the Soviet Union. A new order will certainly arise from these new geopolitical interactions, and not by design, political decision, or by threat of force. Everything formal will fall, and its place be taken by everything that is popular. But has communism truly died?

I say that the age of the masses has begun to impose itself, as it begins its rapid march, igniting people's feelings and captivating their attention. Everything mentioned at the beginning of this introduction will be achieved. We cannot, however, say that communism has died, for it was never born! We should remember what Hitler said to one of his allies: "We must wait for our victory, even if it comes 360 years late."

Communism has not yet been born, so that we may say that it has died. It was Marxism-Leninism that collapsed; or in fact, Stalinism-Leninism, but why did it collapse? One of the tenets of the Islamic revolution in Iran says that it collapsed because of its atheism, and apostasy, and not for political or economic reasons.

Despite the difficulty in believing this argument because of its metaphysical nature, it is hard to discard this reason arbitrarily. There is no doubt that Gorbachev was one of the greatest enemies of God and advocates of abandoning religion, even though he recognized Him when he gave his farewell address: "God has presented us with many blessings, if we only knew how to use them." Is it not enough that Marxism said that religion was the opiate of the masses, and said that religious or tribal societies cannot progress, that scientific research is not permitted by religion, and thus scientific progress is destined to perish in a religious society? This is natural, since religion is a spiritual, or hidden matter, based on belief in the unseen,[111] while science is a tangible, material matter, based on experience. Therefore, accommodating the two, spiritual and material, tangible and hidden, belief and experience, is not possible. Even Ibn Sina was judged an unbeliever because he said,

111. See Quran, Sura 30, verses 6-7.

"Mountains and valleys were made by natural factors of rising and falling during the earth's past ages." Galileo was condemned by the church to be burned because he said, "From the seen, material, realistic point of view, the earth is round." Thus, Marxism settled the issue to the benefit of the freedom of scientific research, without regarding the *haram and halal*[112] and what lies in between this limit of proscribed and prescribed. For the well person, when he prescribes a medicine for a given disease, does not say that this is medicine but it is forbidden, or could be said to be forbidden from the point of view of a certain religion, not to speak of more than one religion.

In addition to this, there is also something else we must mention about Marxism. It involved the world in "fashionable" practices and institutions such as physical liquidation of class enemies, political assassination of opponents, political prisons and secret police, special courts (imitating the French Revolution). Perhaps this was one of the reasons for its fall. In reality, Marxism is a good student of the bourgeoisie.

112. What is forbidden and permitted, respectively, in Islamic law and custom.

What was the 1917 Russian Revolution, if not a good student of the 1789 French Revolution? It is incorrect and unfair to ascribe physical liquidation of class enemies to Marxism; the French bourgeois was the inventor of that practice, when it did away with the feudal class. What were Lenin and Stalin other than pupils of Robespierre and Danton? The left was erroneously ascribed to the communist revolution; the left is actually a child of the French.

The Jacobin extremist revolutionaries were the ones who sat on the left of the French National Assembly hall by accident one day, and the moderates sat on the right: thus the revolutionaries were called the left, and the moderates the right. Thus, the words "left" and "right" come of the dictionary of the French revolution, and not the Russian. As for assassinating opponents, Stalin did not invent this when he had Trotsky assassinated; this was a Roman practice. The assassination of Julius Caesar proves this. The political prison was created by the feudalists; history records the story of Dr. Manet, who forgot his name upon leaving prison, which he had entered a physician and exited a carpenter. Feudalists, before the bourgeoisie, created the secret police; the French revolutionaries, before the precision of the feudalist regime's secret police, were forced to write their lists by using embroidery on fabric, in fear of being caught.

Special, exceptional, and revolutionary courts were also the creation of the French Revolution, and began with the trial and execution of King Louis the XVIth and his wife Marie Antoinette; they were revolutionary at first, then lasted throughout the Terror that was led by the Jacobins.

The cat that devoured its children was not the Bolshevik Revolution; this saying accompanied the French Revolution, which ended with the execution of its leaders Robespierre, Danton, and Saint-Just.

The invention of external and national security and the creation of an official security apparatus were not the province of the Soviet Revolution at all; on the contrary, the Soviet Revolution isolated itself from the world, and created an iron curtain hiding itself, or hiding the world from itself. These things were the creation of the American Revolution. American intelligence still practices this specialty today, in the name of protecting the national and external security of the United States of America. The demagogic rush toward the opponent was the basis of the French Revolution, when it began to march on the feudalists' palaces. The colour red is not the colour of the Bolshevik Revolution, but was first the colour of the French Revolution, before being followed by the Russian.

French history notes that when Marquez passed through one of the streets of Paris on a cart filled with glass barrels filled with wine, and one of them fell and broke on the pavement, the poor flocked around and began to lap up the drink with pieces of fabric. A revolutionary dipped his finger in the red wine and wrote "blood" on a nearby wall, and everyone then knew what that meant.

The abolition of religion was not part of the Russian Revolution's philosophy, but of the French Revolution. It officially abolished Christianity, replacing it with worship of the republic and the souls of the martyrs for freedom.

The Russian Revolution also abolished religion, imitating the French. Thus the Russian Revolution is merely a pupil of the French Revolution in all things, its complete copy. It imitated it in detail; the Russian Revolution brought nothing new with it in the way of these tragedies, or benefits. So, what remained of the Russian Revolution, if the left was imported from the French, as well as revolutionary courts, political prison, solitary confinement, physical liquidation, liquidation of a class, popular army, ideological army—the army formed by the French Revolution to combat royalist Europe—even the colour red is also imported from the French Revolution. What, then, is the communist revolution which we say has fallen? What is the Marxist-Leninist regime that has failed? What ideology has ended? What was the Soviet Union itself that collapsed?

What was the dangerous secret behind this frightening collapse? In reality, the Russian Revolution was nothing but imitation and importation; it was dazzled by the French Revolution, so the revolutionaries of Czarist Russia tried to apply the same in their country. Marxism-Leninism is a nationalist falsehood propagated so that it could not be said that Russia was the pupil of France. There was no Marxism-Leninism, but Robespierrism-Dantonism-Rousseauism. It was not a proletarian revolutionarism; this is another historical falsehood. It was a bourgeois revolution against the feudalist class, exactly like the French Revolution against feudalism. Czarist Russia was a feudalist empire in the true sense of the word. The October Revolution removed that royal feudalism and transformed it into a bourgeois republic, under whose banner was of course collected everything not feudalist, even the poor to the sons of the middle class.

Exactly in the same way that the French Revolution transformed France from a feudalist monarchy to a bourgeois republic with no ideology, merely a revolution of the poorest classes against the feudal class, there was no communist revolution so that we may say that a communist revolution has failed. Communism has not arrived as yet. And it may never come, since it is an imaginary, utopian idea, which has as a condition the existence of a communist man, and this is an impossibility.

The Soviet Union which collapsed is a nationalist struggle which is not foreign to history, but is rather the strongest engine of history, and a former of the map of the world. Whether the Soviet Union was Marxist, capitalist, or anything else, the nationalist struggle that arose was inevitable. It is an inevitable struggle in any country made up of a number of nationalities, such as India, America, and Yugoslavia.

As for those who ruled in Eastern Europe and the former Soviet Union, they were bourgeois parties that turned into, with the passing of time, an aristocratic class. What happened is not strange: it was a very natural thing, although *the greater part of them know it not.*[113]

Therefore, which of the remaining disasters can be attributed to Marxism, so that we may say they were responsible for its collapse? There is only one remaining misfortune in this list of social and political disasters that can truly be ascribed to the Marxist revolution, and this is the economic issue.

113. Referring to a sign from God; Quran, Sura 6, verse 37.

Everything connected to property, its acquisition, its appropriation, sequestration, pricing, subsidizing primary goods, abolishing the law of supply and demand—this is all the result of the Bolshevik Revolution.

So, was this the secret of its fall? Perhaps! Now, following the abolition of so-called socialism, the prices of primary goods have doubled many times over in the Russian republic and the Ukraine, in the countries of Eastern Europe. Columns of beggars have appeared: the achievement of following market policies.

Once Again,
An Urgent Call
to Form a Party

The sinners rejoiced,[114] and the defrauders[115] have shaken hands. Every oathmonger[116] has now become happy, every lowborn hinderer of the good.[117] They thought that they were not responsible, and that the gullible ones would lose. They did not realize that justice is never vanquished in the end; they thought that they had got away with what they had plundered—

114. See Quran, Sura 6, verse 44.
115. See Quran, Sura 83, verse 1.
116. Reference to Quran, Sura 68, verse 10.
117. Reference to Quran, Sura 68, verses 13-14.

that justice can become obsolete over time; they wade with the waders.[118] They became content with what they stole and said that Judgment Day will never come, and said that it was a lie.[119]

He who joins a party betrays Chapter One of the Green Book. The politically forbidden party is a tool of rule which the authorities use on behalf of the people. The party is authority, which belongs to everyone. This is the line of the poem: authority is for all. This sentence is the justification for the call to form a party.

Yes, because authority is for all. In applying the Green Book, we see the necessity of forming a party in order to achieve popular democracy and finally free ourselves of all of the tools of dictatorial rule which plunder the capabilities of the people, and drain the masses of all of their energy and effectiveness. We are in the most urgent need of forming a party, without any delay. Parties are made up of those sharing either the same interests, or the same vision... the same

118. As in fighting on the side of corruption; see Quran, Sura 74, verse 45.
119. Reference to Quran, Sura 2, verse 30ff.

cultural background, or the same place and same ideology.

Those people form a party to achieve their interests, etc. It is not possible in democratic terms for any of them to rule an entire people. The party is a minority of the people, and as long as this is so, then a party must be formed to do away with the rule of a minority over the people.

There is absolutely no contradiction in this logic from the political and revolutionary standpoints, but there is only an apparent contradiction in terms of terminology. In order to understand this formal problematic, and become convinced that it is inevitably necessary to form a party to achieve direct popular democracy, we must submit reality and analyse it.

Today, it is a party and not the people who rules. There are no popular conferences! Therefore, we must crush this tool, which does not represent the people, so that the people can rule. But what is the people? In revolutionary ideological terms, the people is a vague ivory tower[120] term, no clearer than the phrase "the people are the lord of all." For who is this "all" for whom the people act as lord, and is it true that "the people are the lord of all"?

We are now addressing the problem of the meaning of the word "people"(the people is "all citizens," and this is the correct and proper meaning of the word. In this way, we may arrive at the truth, and at the problem that we wish to solve.

Citizens, the totality of which form the people, are peasants, workers, merchants, whether former or current, and former or current middlemen! Black market merchants, former and present employers! Students, government workers, officers, health workers, popular committee members. Travelling salesmen, freethinkers, and smugglers! Illiterate mosque preachers and passport officials and their friends, men—and women—of the customs department,

120. In this collection, Qaddafi uses a pun in Arabic— "bourjaji" instead of "burjwazi" to refer to "bourgeois." "Bourjaji" is his own invention, playing on the ending "aji," which means "ivory," to form a word mocking Marxist terminology, approximating something like "ivory tower bourgeoisie." Since this term is too unwieldy elsewhere in the text, it is used sparingly.

airport and guest lounge employees and their friends, soldiers who obtain their pay, and those who do not—all of them make up the people. Added to this are those receiving treatment abroad, and those who are not allowed to receive treatment abroad, for non-health-related reasons! Also, those who have received telephones and those who have not received them, due to a lack of information.

The people is also made up of those who are abroad to undertake certain missions, and those who travel abroad several times a year, and have no business to undertake. This definition of the people does not distinguish between those, when abroad, who stay in Intercontinental Hotels or sleep in Libyan embassies until their mission is finished, and then return home.

This entire mixture makes up the people, with the exception of Moroccan, Ethiopian, and Filipina servants, since "people should do their own housework" and "the child is raised by his mother."[121] The definition of the people also

---

121. Maxims taken from the Green Book, which in the Libyan Arab Socialist Jamahiriyya has a constitutional power.

includes military, political, and revolutionary lea-
derships, their relatives and friends, the friends of
their friends, relatives, and *the attendants who
follow them in kindness*[122] until Judgement Day![123]

In order to produce a fair and scientific
definition of "the people," we should note that it
also includes university professors, doctors,
teachers, people living in Ghout al-Shammal, Abi
Salim, al-Fallah, Sirte, Tobruk, al-Joush, and
Mazzada, with the exception of the Dao people,
for they are of Korean origin, and natural healing
nurses, for they are of Slavic origin.

This definition of the people includes all
of those with suitcases full of clothes, and those
without. Those who pass through inspection
lines, and those who do not. A citizen is a
citizen, whether or not he can import a car,
whether or not he has chauffeur, and as the
saying goes, "the car belongs to the driver." You
are counted to be a citizen and part of the
people, whether or not you have a swimming
pool or a yacht. Whether or not a tailor comes

122. Quran, Sura 2, verse 178.
123. Or, the "day of paying back debts."

to you or you go to the tailor.

This, then, is the definition of "the people." It means every citizen who lives in the Idriss housing project in Abi Salim or still lives in a tent in the Bi valley, or those who live in Abu Nuwwas neighbourhood, or those who go to Switzerland with their spouses, or merely go to their spouses at the end of each day. Citizenship has no relationship with marriage or bachelorhood. We have now laid out the definition of "the people," and it has become clear to us that it is a truly bourgeois definition, and quite unsatisfying. It is a mixture of contradictions and speculations. No doubt, in this definition, "the people" includes sections of the population that are hostile to one another, combative elements, groups that are against each other socially. Thus, within a people, there are forces and elements of exploitation, theft and monopoly, as well as partisanship, tribalism, reaction, and corruption.

Following this definition of "the people," we return to our call for the forming of a party, but how? Those who rule now, under an umbrella of popular democracy, are not the masses,

building a state of the masses, but an alliance—
not of the people's labouring forces—but an
alliance that is against them. It is a despicable
alliance, whose own elements do not know one
another, but they know each other's
methods. They do not meet together and take an
oath of allegiance: their alliance is a tacit one.[124]
This is the party that rules today. However, do
not fear them to the degree that you count them
all allied against you, for they actually hate one
another, being as they fight one another in their
garbage heaps. There is no option but to form a
new party—not a party to rule the people, but to
draw out the masses from within the people. Not
a partial party that rules the entirety, but an
entirety that produces a part—the body trium-
phing over the cancer.

It is a daring operation, a qualitative leap, a
new revolutionary lead to create the state of the
masses. Only the masses have an interest in
revolution, which the parasites take their share
of, and Dracula drinks its blood.

O unknown ones, good-hearted ones, you

124. See Quran, Sura 59, verse 14.

who do not know who provides you with
telephones, who do not know who exempts you
from paying your monthly bills, you who live
in an old, run-down house in the shadow of an
imposing palace. You who do not know who
sends you abroad for medical treatment, who do
not know how you obtained a car or how you
received—and not at your own expense—an
airline ticket. O non-bourgeois citizens,
hardworking ones, sweating toiling ones, O
widows, and divorcees, in contravention of
Islamic law. You who have been raped by
money, you silent, defeated women, you who
have no one to speak for you, only God has the
power. You who have left pleasures, who was
forced to leave home, you who know no one
and are known by none. You soldiers stationed
on the front, you cleaning ladies and street
sweepers, you loyal teachers, you whose hands
are stained by lime, tar, dust, mud, or salt, or
the blood of operations or killing. All of you
with rough hands ("The rough hand is loved by
God and His Prophet." You who have been
forced to become a chauffeur for an idle, ivory
tower woman; you who have been forced to ride
alone in the front, wash the expensive car with
fresh water, while drinking salt water in your

home. You to whom it has been said: consume
the most delicious of food and drink[125]—while
at home you lack even drinking water. You know
that authority belongs to you but you remain
silent, know that the revolution is for you yet you
remain patiently waiting. You who know that we
love you but you are unable to reach us, you who
love us, but are unable to reach us.

O listless ones, O leaderless ones, O poor
ones. This is your age, the age of the masses. This
is your revolution, the popular revolution. This is
your path, the green path has been opened. This
is your Green Book, take it up with firm
resolve[126] and read what it contains twice, thrice,
and four times. It is your historical opportunity
to rule and be sovereign; to walk your path
joyfully. You will cross the earth and conquer the
highest mountains. Disregard the advice of the
sage Luqman to his son; this is not your concern.
This is another age, the age of the masses. March
forward. Beat down the earth with your broken,
naked feet. It was created for you. Raise your
heads high to the sky, it was made beautiful for
your sakes. Raise your voices; there are no more

125. See Quran, Sura 25, verse 53.
126. Reference to Quran, Sura 19, verse 12.

prophets before which you should lower your voices. Shout out what you will as loud as you can. The goddess whom you used to fear is dead, so cast out your loneliness. We killed her on the great day of the revolution, the day of the Zawara speech. The sixth anniversary of the revolution, on midnight of Tuesday the 6-7th of October and the month Fatih, 1978.

I swear to you that the goddess is dead, and her justice with her. Her prophets with her as well. We have seen the death of the last prophet. All that remains is God *the glorified, the high exalted,*[127] *the beneficent,*[128] *the merciful, the compassionate, the subtle*[129] and *the loving.*[130]

All of this acts to remove the fear[131] from our hearts, strengthens our freedom, and confirms are power over the earth. If you encounter a god, slay it and crucify it. If you encounter a prophet, curse him and kill him.

127. See Quran, Sura 17, verse 43.
128. See Quran, Sura 55, verse 17.
129. See Quran, Sura 6, verse 103.
130. See Quran, Sura 10, verse 90.
131. Implicit reference to several Quranic verses: Sura 7, verse 154; Sura 2, verse 40; Sura 16, verse 51; Sura 8, verse 60.

They are charlatans and liars. The goddess is dead and so is her prophet. Do not believe if one says to you: I am god or a prophet; he is false. He is a false prophet, a Musaylima, Sajjah.[132] The world belongs to all; the house to its inhabitant, the car to the driver; he who produces consumes his production. People should do their own housework. A child is raised by its mother. The university is for its students, the school for its pupils. Authority, wealth, and arms are for all. And to you all goes out the call for the masses to begin lining up on the left; let their opponents stand on the right and let the barricades go up between them.

So that the work can proceed, so that words be matched by deeds, my friends, go out toward the revolutionary paths. Record your names and addresses; you will find the membership ledger open to all.[133] For you, O hypocrites, you who have disfigured every holy revolutionary struggle. O capricious ones, O chameleons, do not try this time to do what you did in the past, if only for one simple reason—this time we know you. If any of you step forward and try to mix with us, as you

132. False prophets killed in battle by the first caliph.
133. See footnote 124.

were used to doing in the past, *I verily will punish him the punishment of the hoopoe, and verily will slay him*[134] following a long torment, you have in front of you another door to take. Do not register your names with hours, but register what is in your conscience. You must either confess, or not confess, but what is right and what is wrong are both clear. The right path is clear, and once again, the warning bell has rung.

Forgive the one who warns you of misfortune.[135]

---

134. See Quran, Sura 27, verse 21.
135. An expression roughly equivalent to "do not blame the bearer of bad tidings."